Wild Sides

An A–Z of essential, exceptional vegetable side dishes

Vicki Wild

 HarperCollins*Publishers*

HarperCollins *Publishers*

First published in Australia in 2005
by HarperCollins *Publishers* Pty Limited
ABN 36 009 913 517
A member of the HarperCollins *Publishers* (Australia) Pty Limited Group
www.harpercollins.com.au

HarperCollins *Publishers*
25 Ryde Road, Pymble, Sydney, NSW 2073, Australia
31 View Road, Glenfield, Auckland 10, New Zealand
77–85 Fulham Palace Road, London W6 8JB, United Kingdom
2 Bloor Street East, 20th floor, Toronto, Ontario M4W 1A8, Canada
10 East 53rd Street, New York NY 10022, USA

National Library of Australia Cataloguing-in-Publication data:

Wild, Vicki.
  Wild sides.
  ISBN 0 7322 6846 X.
  1. Cookery (Vegetables). I. Title.
641.65

Art direction and design by Mark Gowing Design
Photography by Richard Mortimer
Produced by Phoenix Offset on 120gsm Woodfree
Printed in China

5 4 3 2 1   05 06 07 08

Contents

These days it's so hard to tell when vegetables are in season, because most vegetables — especially the common ones — are available all year round. However, there is no doubt that vegetables in season taste better. It makes sense; they have usually travelled less than those flown in from around the world. (And they often cost less.)

Local produce nearly always tastes better, particularly if you can purchase directly from a farmer. If you are buying from a local greengrocer or supermarket, you can ask where the vegetables come from or check the box the vegetables came in.

Organic?

In order for a farm to be certified as organic, the farm must use only organic farming methods for three years before the organic certification is made. All foods labelled as organic must come from organic farms. This means that the farm uses a minimum of synthetic fertilisers and pesticides and no antibiotics or hormones. It does not mean pesticide free. Producers are still allowed to select from a limited list of pesticides that have been used for a long period.

Approximate vegetable seasons

Artichoke	June to November
Asparagus (imported)	October to February & January to June
Butter Beans	December to May
Flat Beans	all year, peaking June to August
Broad Beans	June to October
Beetroot	all year, peaking June to November
Bok Choy	all year, peaking May to August
Broccoli	all year, peaking June to November
Cabbage	all year, peaking September to January
Capsicum	all year
Carrot	all year, peaking April to August
Cauliflower	all year, peaking June to September
Celeriac	March to December
Celery	all year, peaking January to August

Corn	all year, peaking September to March	Shallot	all year
		Silverbeet	all year
Eggplant	all year, peaking November to March	Snake Bean	all year, peaking July to April
Fennel	March to October	Snow Pea	all year, peaking July to October
Green Beans	all year, peaking November to March		
		Spinach	March to November
Jerusalem Artichoke	April to October	Squash	all year, peaking November to March
Leek	all year, peaking October to May	Sweet Potato	all year
		Tomato	all year, peaking November to February
Lettuce	all year, peaking November to March		
		Turnip	all year, peaking April to September
Mushroom	all year		
Onion	all year	Witlof	all year, peaking May to October
Parsnip	all year		
Peas	all year, peaking October to December	Zucchini	all year, peaking November to January
Potato	all year		
Pumpkin	all year, peaking February to May		
Radish	all year, peaking October to December		

This seasonal chart is intended to serve as a guide only. Fresh produce varies from state to state and region to region.

Courtesy of Sydney Markets

Boiling and Simmering

Boiling and simmering entail cooking vegetables in a liquid, usually water or stock. Boiling requires cooking at 100°C, whereas simmering is just below boiling point, at between 95°C and 98°C. Boiling and simmering are quick and convenient methods, but simmering is less likely to toughen the flesh.

Equipment

Any large, deep cooking pot that will hold the vegetables with sufficient liquid is suitable.

How to boil and simmer

Vegetables can be boiled or simmered in salted water or any suitable stock. Use enough liquid to cover the vegetables completely. As a guide, the liquid should be four times the volume of the vegetables. Place the vegetables into the boiling liquid, and bring back to the boil. Reduce to a simmer and cook, covered, for the desired amount of time. Drain immediately.

Steaming

Steaming cooks the vegetables by the heat of the steam, at a temperature higher than 100°C, and is suitable for most vegetables that can be boiled. Steaming is a great method for retaining nutrients in vegetables; however, steaming takes somewhat longer than boiling.

Equipment

Bamboo steaming basket with a lid, placed over a wok or saucepan; stainless-steel saucepan with perforated steaming pan and lid; steaming oven; or conventional oven using baking paper or an aluminium foil parcel.

How to steam

Bring liquid to the boil. Place the vegetables in a single layer on the perforated surface of the steamer. Cover tightly and steam. Check the vegetables at regular intervals to avoid overcooking.

If using a liquid marinade, place the vegetables on a plate that will fit easily inside the steamer. Allow sufficient room around the plate for the steam to rise.

Vegetables can be steamed over plain water; however, adding herbs or citrus will add a subtle flavour.

Approximate boiling and steaming times

Artichoke (whole) (whole)	baby: 15 minutes medium: 15–20 minutes large: 20–25 minutes		Corn	with husk: 10 minutes without husk: 7 minutes
Asparagus	small: 1–2 minutes medium: 3–5 minutes large: 8–12 minutes		Parsnip	15–20 minutes
			Peas	baby: 1 minute older: 3–4 minutes
Beans	fresh shelled: 10–20 minutes dried shelled: 1–3 hours		Potato	small: 15–20 minutes medium: 20–25 minutes large: 25–35 minutes
Beetroot	baby: 20 minutes medium: 30 minutes large: 1 hour or more		Pumpkin	cut into chunks: 10–15 minutes
			Spinach	30 seconds
Bok Choy	stems: 8 minutes leaves: 4 minutes		String Beans	thick: 5–10 minutes French type: 4–6 minutes
Broccoli	3–5 minutes		Sweet Potato	peeled and cut into chunks: 30 minutes
Cabbage	10–20 minutes		Turnip	peeled and cut into chunks: 15–20 minutes
Carrot	cut into pieces: 6–8 minutes whole: 10–12 minutes		Zucchini	cut into chunks: 3–5 minutes
Cauliflower	5 minutes			

Roasting, baking and braising are simple and effective methods for cooking vegetables. Roasting is usually done with the vegetables uncovered in an oven between 180°C and 220°C; baking vegetables requires covering and cooking at between 140°C and 230°C; and braising usually involves covering and cooking on a range-top or in an oven between 180°C and 220°C.

Roasting, baking and braising are healthy ways of cooking, as little oil or fat needs to be used. These methods can give the outside of vegetables a crispy, golden coating while maintaining the moisture inside.

Roasting and baking are suitable for most starchy vegetables such as potatoes, pumpkins and sweet potatoes as well as other moist, densely textured vegetables such as tomatoes, beetroots, eggplants, onions and turnips.

Most vegetables with enough moisture can be roasted or baked. However, for small green vegetables (such as peas and beans) the drying effects of the oven and the long cooking time make roasting or baking undesirable.

Braising is suitable for most vegetables. It takes longer than boiling or simmering; however, the result is a much more complex and intense flavour.

Equipment
An oven and a suitable baking pan or dish; or a kettle barbecue.

How to roast and bake
Place the vegetables in an oiled baking dish in a single layer and baste the top of the vegetables with oil, butter or marinade. Cook in a pre-heated oven, and turn at regular intervals during cooking.

How to braise
Aromatic seasonings and stocks added to the vegetables is a perfect way to braise: place the vegetables in a baking dish in a single layer, pour in the stocks and seasonings, and cook over a low heat. Baste the vegetables at regular intervals during cooking.

The flavoured cooking liquid is served with the vegetables. The liquid can be drained off and reduced over high heat before serving to concentrate the flavour.

Approximate roasting times and temperatures

Asparagus	180°C – 220°C	15 minutes
Beetroot	160°C – 200°C	30 minutes–1 hour for baby beetroots 1–1½ hours for large beetroots
Carrot	180°C – 200°C	40–50 minutes
Fennel	180°C – 190°C	30–40 minutes when cut into halves or quarters
Garlic	180°C – 200°C	35 minutes (whole head)
Mushroom	200°C – 250°C	20 minutes
Onion	190°C – 220°C	40 minutes for small onions 1½ hours for large onions
Parsnip	190°C – 200°C	45 minutes when halved or quartered 1½ hours when whole
Potato	180°C – 220°C	30–45 minutes
Sweet Potato	190°C – 200°C	50 minutes
Tomato	150°C – 160°C 190°C – 200°C	1½ hours for small or cherry tomatoes 2–2½ hours for large tomatoes
Turnip	180°C – 220°C	40 minutes – 1 hour when cut into chunks
Zucchini	180°C – 200°C	40 minutes when small or cut into sections

Barbecuing and grilling are dry heat methods in which the heat source comes from only one direction. Heating from above is from a salamander or oven grill and heating from below is from a grill plate or char grill. Barbecuing and grilling are fast and simple methods to cook vegetables while adding a distinctive flavour and appearance.

Barbecuing and grilling are suitable for most vegetables, but some vegetables (such as artichokes and fennel) won't cook through on the grill and have to be steamed or simmered for a few minutes before they are barbecued. For delicate vegetables, cover the grill plate with aluminium foil that has been perforated, lest they dry out and fall apart when placed on intense heat. Any raw vegetable that is basted or marinated is great on the grill.

Equipment
Charcoal barbecue; electric barbecue; gas barbecue; char grill plate; or salamander or oven grill.

How to barbecue or grill
Try marinating vegetables for a few minutes before grilling by tossing in olive oil and some chopped fresh herbs such as thyme, oregano, rosemary or marjoram. Marinating the vegetables before barbecuing or grilling enhances the flavour and protects the flesh from drying out.

Brush the grill plate with oil to prevent vegetables from sticking. An electric grill should be set at a medium–high heat, whereas a gas grill should have a medium heat.

Slice or section the vegetables, baste with olive oil, butter or marinade and grill directly over the heat.

Smaller vegetables can be threaded onto steel or wooden skewers. Push the pieces together so that the flavours blend and the flesh holds together. Then baste the vegetables with oil or marinade and place on the grill.

Avoid using too much oil to baste the vegetables as the oil can drip down over the coals and cause flames. The easiest way to avoid this is to move the vegetables around the grill and take them off as soon as you see any flames.

Delicate herbs such as basil, parsley and tarragon should be tossed over the vegetables as soon as they come off the grill, as these herbs will lose some of their flavour if exposed to direct heat.

Preparation and cooking times for barbecuing and grilling

Artichoke
To prepare, simmer artichoke bottoms or baby artichokes in a pot of salted water for 15 minutes, or until tender. Slice artichoke bottoms into quarters and baby artichokes into halves lengthwise. To cook, toss with olive oil and fresh herbs and grill for 5–6 minutes. If using skewers, turn the artichokes frequently.

Asparagus
To prepare, slice off the woody end and discard. If the asparagus is thick, and the skin is tough, remove the bottom 3–4 cm of skin. To cook, toss lightly in olive oil and grill for 4–5 minutes.

Capsicum
To prepare, halve the capsicums lengthwise, remove the seeds and stems, then cut into strips or thread small sections onto skewers. To cook, grill until the skins start to blister and blacken, turning frequently. Place the grilled capsicum in a plastic bag or cover with cling film for about 10 minutes to sweat; the skins will remove easily.

Corn on the cob
These can be grilled with or without the husks. To grill with husks, peel back the husks and keep intact. Remove the silks and then fold the husks back in place. Secure with string. The string will burn away over the grill. If the husks are remaining, dip the cob in water briefly and place on the hot grill for 15 minutes, turning frequently. For corn with the husks removed, brush lightly with olive oil and grill for 5–6 minutes or until lightly browned.

Eggplant
To prepare, slice off the ends and cut into rounds or lengthwise into strips. Brush lightly with olive oil and season with salt and pepper. To cook, grill for 5–6 minutes or until lightly browned on each side.

Fennel
To prepare, trim off the base of the fennel and remove any of the stringy foliage and any small stalks. The fennel can be sliced into halves or quarters. To cook, brush lightly with olive oil and grill over a low to medium heat for 5 minutes (depending on size) each side.

Mushroom

Very little preparation is required for mushrooms. For the more common cap varieties, remove the stems; a damp cloth can be used to wipe away any dirt. To cook smaller mushrooms, thread onto skewers, brush lightly with olive oil and place on the grill for 2–3 minutes, turning frequently. Keep larger mushrooms whole, brush with a little olive oil and grill for 4–5 minutes, turning frequently. Grill until just golden.

Onion

To prepare, peel the skin from onions and slice into rounds, strips or quarters. Onion quarters can be threaded onto skewers with a variety of vegetables. Lightly brush with olive oil and grill for 4–5 minutes or until golden. Toss onion rounds or strips in a little olive oil and grill for 4–5 minutes or until golden.

Potato

To prepare, place whole unpeeled potatoes in salted cold water. Slowly bring to the boil and simmer for 15–20 minutes, or until tender. Drain well and allow to cool. Peel the potatoes when cooled and cut into halves or quarters. Then brush lightly with olive oil and grill over medium heat for 5–6 minutes or until golden, turning regularly.

Sweet Potato

To prepare, cut unpeeled sweet potatoes into chunks and place in salted cold water. Slowly bring to the boil and simmer for 15–20 minutes, or until just tender. Drain well and allow to cool. Peel the sweet potato when cooled and cut into halves or quarters. Then brush lightly with olive oil and grill over medium heat for 5–6 minutes or until golden, turning regularly.

Witlof

To prepare, remove any dark or damaged outer leaves. Cut the witlof into halves or quarters lengthwise through to the root end. To cook, toss lightly in olive oil and grill flat side down first for 5–6 minutes, turning regularly.

Zucchini

To prepare, trim the ends from the zucchini and cut into thick slices lengthwise. To cook, brush with olive oil or marinade and grill for 3–4 minutes or until lightly browned on both sides.

Pan-frying, Stir-frying and Deep-frying

Deep-frying and pan-frying vegetables in oils or butter are relatively fast methods and easily controlled, and suit almost all vegetables.

Deep-frying and pan-frying are ideal for finishing off pre-cooked or blanched vegetables as well as completely cooking vegetables from the raw state.

Equipment
A thermostatically controlled deep-fryer or wok, for deep-frying; any flat, heavy based pan, for pan-frying; or a wok or large based pan, for stir-frying.

How to pan-fry, stir-fry and deep-fry
When pan-frying, add oil or butter (or a mixture of both) to the pan. Once the pan is heated, place the vegetables presentation side down and cook over medium to high heat. The cooking time will vary depending on the thickness of the vegetables.

Stir-frying requires vegetables to be cut into thin equal-sized pieces for fast and even cooking. Add the ingredients in the order of the longest cooking time first; this way all ingredients will be ready at the same time.

Deep-frying vegetables in clean hot oil between 170°C and 180°C is best when vegetables have a coating such as flour, breadcrumbs or batter. To test the heat of the oil, place a small amount of batter or bread in hot oil – it should sizzle and turn golden within 30 seconds. The coating seals in the moisture and stops the oil entering the vegetables.

When deep-frying, cook only a small amount at a time by lowering the vegetables into oil with tongs or in a frying basket. When cooked, drain excess oil on absorbent kitchen paper.

Pan-fried Artichokes
with Basil and Pine Nuts

4 large artichokes
lemon juice and salt for blanching
4 tablespoons olive oil
2 cloves garlic, roughly chopped
1 cup roughly chopped basil leaves
½ cup pine nuts, toasted

1 Trim the stalks of each artichoke, leaving approximately 4 cm attached. Peel the remaining stalk. Remove tough outer leaves and discard. 2 Blanch in water with lemon juice and a little salt. 3 Cook for 5 minutes or until just tender. Drain. 4 Cut the artichokes into quarters lengthwise and set aside. 5 Heat the oil in a frying pan over medium heat, add the garlic and cook until golden. 6 Add the artichoke and sauté until the outsides are just browned. 7 Stir through the basil leaves and pine nuts.

Serving idea
Serve with Roasted Tomatoes
recipe, page 131

Roasted Artichoke Hearts
filled with Olives and Capers

4 large artichoke hearts, trimmed

1 large lemon, halved

½ cup olive oil

2 cloves garlic, minced

2 cups fresh, coarse breadcrumbs

3 tablespoons roughly chopped
    flat-leaf parsley

2 tablespoons roughly chopped thyme

2 tablespoons kalamata olives,
    pitted and chopped

2 tablespoons capers, rinsed and drained

1 tablespoon red wine vinegar

1 small tomato, diced

80 grams ricotta cheese

1 large onion, finely chopped

salt

pepper

¼ cup white wine

1 Preheat the oven to 180°C. 2 Rub the trimmed artichokes well with half of the lemon. 3 With a spoon or melon-baller, hollow out each artichoke. 4 Juice the remaining half lemon. 5 Add the lemon juice to ¾ litre of water, add the artichokes and set aside until ready to roast. 6 For the filling, add ¼ cup of the oil to a frying pan over medium heat. Add the garlic and breadcrumbs, and cook until crisp and golden. 7 Add the parsley, thyme, olives and capers. 8 Add the vinegar and tomato. Add the ricotta, season to taste with salt and pepper, and combine well. 9 Remove the artichokes from the water and drain. 10 Divide the stuffing among the hollowed-out artichokes. 11 In a frying pan, add the remaining oil and sauté the onion over medium heat until tender and golden. 12 Season the onion to taste with salt and pepper and spread evenly over the base of a baking dish large enough to hold the artichokes. 13 Place the artichokes on the onion and pour the wine into the dish. 14 Cover with foil and cook until heated through, about 25 minutes. 15 Remove the foil, baste with a little oil and cook until the tops are brown.

Serving idea
Serve with salad leaves

Warm Salad of Artichoke Hearts
with Peas and Rocket

4 large, raw artichoke hearts, trimmed
250 grams fresh peas, shelled
8 tablespoons olive oil
4 cloves garlic, peeled and crushed
¼ teaspoon sea salt
¾ cup water or vegetable stock
   (recipe, page 152)
4 tablespoons white wine
½ cup roughly chopped flat-leaf parsley
2 tablespoons lemon juice
freshly ground black pepper
1 bunch rocket leaves

1 Cut the artichoke hearts crossways into thick slices. 2 Bring a saucepan of water to the boil, add the peas and cook until just tender. Rinse, drain and set aside. 3 Heat the oil in a large frying pan over medium heat. Add the garlic and artichoke hearts, and cook until just golden. 4 Add the salt, stock and wine, and gently bring to the boil. 5 Reduce the heat to low, cover the pan and gently simmer until the artichokes are tender. 6 Add the peas, parsley, lemon juice, black pepper and a little more sea salt. 7 Add the rocket leaves and toss through gently.

Serving idea
Serve with grilled fish or roasted potatoes

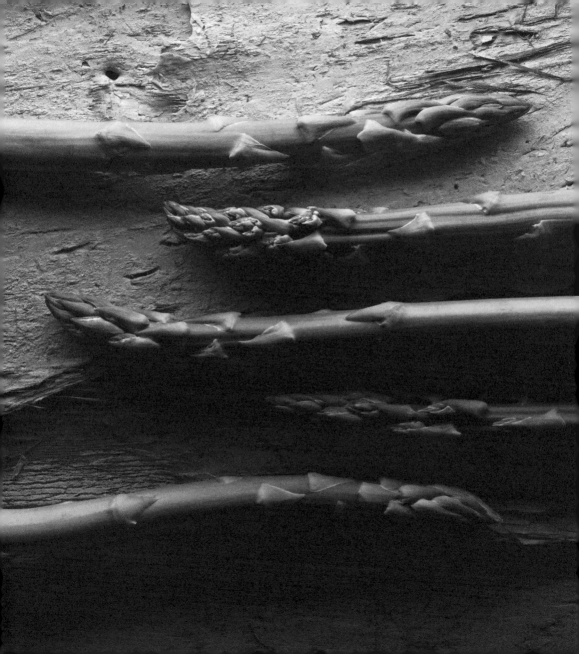

250 grams dried soba noodles
1 tablespoon lime juice
1 tablespoon light soy sauce
1 teaspoon mirin
½ teaspoon sugar
⅓ cup grapeseed oil
2 bunches asparagus, trimmed and sliced
12 snow peas, julienned
2 cloves garlic, minced
2 medium spring onions, finely chopped
2 tablespoons black sesame seeds

1 Place the noodles in a saucepan of boiling water. When the water returns to the boil, add an additional cup of cold water and continue to boil for 8 minutes or until al dente. 2 Drain and set aside to cool.
3 For the dressing, combine the lime juice, soy sauce, mirin and sugar. Mix together well. 4 Pour in the grapeseed oil and stir to combine well. 5 In a frying pan, add a little extra grapeseed oil and heat over medium heat. Add the garlic and fry until golden. Add the asparagus and sauté until tender.
6 Toss through the snow peas and cook for a further 30 seconds. 7 Remove from the heat. 8 Toss the noodles in the dressing. Place the noodles on a serving plate and pour over the asparagus and snow peas.
9 Garnish with the spring onion and black sesame seeds and serve.

Serving idea
Serve with sashimi or seared tuna

Steamed Asparagus
with Asian Vinaigrette

2 bunches asparagus, trimmed and sliced

4 teaspoons light soy sauce
1 teaspoon caster sugar
1 teaspoon Chinese rice wine
2 teaspoons red wine vinegar
1 teaspoon sesame oil
2 cloves garlic, minced
1 small red chilli, finely chopped

1 Bring a large saucepan of water to a simmer. Add the asparagus and cook for 1–2 minutes or until just tender. 2 Drain and set aside to cool. 3 In a bowl, combine the remaining ingredients. 4 When ready to serve, place the asparagus on a serving plate and pour over the dressing.

Serving idea
Serve with barbecued scallops and steamed rice

Stir-fried Asparagus
with Shiitake Mushrooms

2 bunches asparagus, trimmed
6 medium shiitake mushrooms,
    stems removed
4 tablespoons unsalted butter
⅓ cup finely chopped golden shallots
2 cloves garlic, minced
sea salt
black pepper
¼ cup Chinese rice wine
1 bunch chives, cut into 2 cm lengths

1 Cut the asparagus spears in half, on the diagonal. 2 Cut the shiitake mushrooms into thin slices. 3 Melt the butter over a medium heat in a wok or large frying pan. Add the shallots and garlic, and cook until golden. 4 Add the asparagus and mushrooms, season to taste with salt and black pepper, and stir-fry for 2 minutes or until just tender. 5 Add the wine and simmer for a further 2 minutes. 6 Remove from the heat. 7 Serve immediately, garnished with chives.

Serving idea
Serve with grilled sirloin steaks

400 grams green beans, trimmed
2 tablespoons olive oil
1 tablespoon sherry vinegar
100 grams fetta, crumbled
½ cup walnut halves, toasted
sea salt
cracked black pepper

1 Place the beans in a saucepan of boiling water. Simmer for 2–3 minutes or until tender. 2 Drain, then rinse the beans under cold water. 3 Toss the beans in the oil and vinegar and place on a serving plate. 4 Sprinkle over the fetta and walnuts. 5 Season with salt and pepper.

Serving idea
Serve with barbecued sardines

Buttered Beans with Cashews and Spring Onion

450 grams green beans, trimmed
3 tablespoons butter
1 clove garlic, minced
sea salt
black pepper
1 cup cashews
⅓ cup roughly chopped flat-leaf parsley
1 small spring onion, finely chopped

1 Blanch the beans in a large saucepan of boiling water for 5–6 minutes or until just tender. 2 Remove from the heat and drain well. Set aside. 3 Melt the butter in a frying pan over medium heat, add the garlic and cook until golden. Season to taste with salt and pepper. 4 Add the cashew nuts and sauté until golden. Add the parsley and cook a further 30 seconds. 5 Place the warm beans on a serving plate and pour over the butter mixture. 6 Toss well and garnish with spring onions.

Serving idea
Serve with pan-fried white fish fillets

Snake Beans Braised in Tomato and Basil Sauce

1 large onion, finely chopped
3 cloves garlic, minced
3 tablespoons olive oil
2 x 440 gram tins of chopped tomatoes, with liquid
1 cup roughly chopped basil leaves
450 grams snake beans, trimmed
sea salt
black pepper
2 tablespoons finely chopped parsley

1 Cook the onion and garlic in 1 tablespoon of the olive oil in a large, heavy based saucepan until just golden. 2 Add the tinned tomatoes and basil, and simmer on a high heat until thick and pulpy, about 10 minutes. 3 Add the beans, cover, and cook for a further 10 minutes, stirring every few minutes. 4 When the beans have softened, season with salt and pepper, and cook for a further 5 minutes on a low heat until the sauce coats the beans. 5 Stir in the remaining olive oil and garnish with parsley. 6 Serve immediately.

Serving idea
Serve with roast lamb

Balsamic-roasted Baby Beetroots and Spanish Onion

4 tablespoons olive oil
12 small baby beetroots, cleaned and trimmed
2 large Spanish onions, quartered
2 tablespoons balsamic vinegar
1 pinch caster sugar
1 tablespoon fresh grated horseradish
    or to taste
200 ml sour cream
sea salt

1 Preheat the oven to 220°C. 2 Pour the oil into a baking dish measuring approximately 20 cm x 20 cm. 3 Place the beetroots and onion in the baking dish and toss well in the oil. 4 Drizzle with the vinegar and sprinkle with the pinch of sugar. 5 Roast for 15 minutes or until tender. The beetroots are done when a skewer can be inserted easily but they are still firm. 6 Meanwhile, in a small bowl, add a little of the horseradish to the sour cream. Add more depending on taste. Season with salt. 7 Place the beetroots and onion on a serving plate. 8 Serve immediately with horseradish cream to the side.

Serving idea
Serve with barbecued salmon fillets

1 bunch baby beetroot, trimmed
250 ml natural yoghurt
sea salt
black pepper
2 tablespoons finely chopped mint
2 tablespoons olive oil
2 cloves garlic, minced
½ cup roughly chopped coriander leaves

1 Place the beetroots in a large saucepan of water and bring to the boil. Cook for 30 minutes or until tender. 2 Drain and set aside to cool. 3 When cooled, peel off the skins and discard. 4 Cut the beetroot into small slices and place into a bowl. 5 Put the yoghurt in a separate bowl and season to taste with salt and pepper. Stir in the mint and combine well. 6 Heat the oil in a frying pan over medium heat. Add the garlic and cook until just golden. 7 Remove from the heat and pour over the beetroot. Gently combine. 8 To serve, place the beetroot in a serving bowl and top with a large dollop of minted yoghurt. 9 Garnish with coriander leaves.

Serving idea
Serve with poached ocean trout

4 large beetroots, cleaned and trimmed
1 tablespoon butter
2 large onions, finely chopped
3 sticks celery, finely chopped
1 tablespoon red wine or raspberry vinegar
1 tablespoon finely chopped flat-leaf parsley
2 tablespoons finely chopped coriander leaves
250 ml cream
sea salt
black pepper

1 Place the beetroots in a large saucepan of water and slowly bring to the boil. Simmer for 1½ hours or until tender. 2 Remove from the heat. Drain and rinse under cold water. Peel and discard the skins. 3 Cut the beetroots into small chunks and set aside. 4 Melt the butter in a large, heavy based saucepan. Add the onion and celery and cook until softened, stirring frequently. 5 Add the beetroot, wine, parsley and coriander. Combine well. 6 Pour in enough water to make a thick soup, not covering the vegetables. 7 Simmer for 10 minutes and set aside to cool. 8 Purée the mixture with a hand blender until smooth. 9 Pour in the cream and stir to combine. 10 Season to taste with salt and pepper. 11 Serve chilled.

Serving idea
Serve as a starter

Stir-fried Bok Choy
with Chilli and Oyster Sauce

2 bunches bok choy, stalks trimmed
4 tablespoons oyster sauce
1 teaspoon caster sugar
1 tablespoon peanut oil
2 cloves garlic, minced
1 small green chilli, finely chopped
sea salt
black pepper

1 Separate the bok choy 'branches' and cut in half lengthwise. 2 Rinse and allow to dry well. 3 Cut the stems from the leaves. 4 Combine the oyster sauce and sugar in a small bowl. Set aside. 5 Heat the peanut oil in a wok or frying pan over medium heat, add the garlic and chilli and allow to sizzle for 1 minute. 6 Add the bok choy stems and stir-fry for 3 minutes or until tender. Add the leaves and stir-fry for another minute. 7 Pour in the oyster sauce mixture and toss together for 30 seconds. 8 Season to taste with salt and pepper.

Serving idea
Serve with barbecued white fish fillets

1 tablespoon fermented black beans
1 large broccoli head, cut into florets
3 tablespoons peanut oil
2 cloves garlic, finely chopped
1 tablespoon minced ginger
1 teaspoon caster sugar
½ cup chicken stock
juice of 1 small lemon

1 Cover the black beans with warm water and soak for 10 minutes. 2 Place the broccoli in a large saucepan of boiling water and cook for 2 minutes or until just tender. 3 Remove from the heat and drain thoroughly. 4 Drain the black beans and chop very finely. 5 Heat the peanut oil in a frying pan over medium heat. Add the chopped beans, garlic and ginger. Stir-fry until sizzling. 6 Add the broccoli and coat well with the oil mixture. 7 Add the sugar and stock and stir-fry for another 2 minutes. 8 Stir in the lemon juice and serve immediately.

Serving idea
Serve with hokkien noodles

Broccoli with Roasted Capsicum and Fetta

4 medium, roasted red capsicums
(recipe, page 45)
4 medium roasted yellow capsicums
1 large broccoli head, cut into florets
2 tablespoons olive oil plus extra for serving
3 cloves garlic, minced
juice of ½ lemon
2 tablespoons lemon thyme leaves
100 grams fetta cheese, crumbled
cracked black pepper

1 Slice the roasted capsicums into thin strips and set aside. 2 Place the broccoli in a large saucepan of boiling water and cook until tender. Drain and set aside. 3 Heat the oil in a frying pan over medium heat, add the garlic and cook until just sizzling. Add the capsicum, lemon juice, broccoli and thyme and toss well for 1 minute. 4 Pour the broccoli mixture onto a large serving plate and top with the fetta. 5 To serve, drizzle over a little olive oil and season with cracked black pepper.

Serving idea
Serve with lamb cutlets

400 grams fettuccine
500 grams broccoli, cut into florets
200 grams zucchini, cut into batons
2 cups olive oil
1 large onion, finely chopped
2 cloves garlic, minced
2 small red chillies, finely chopped
juice of ½ medium lemon
sea salt

1 Place the fettuccine in a large saucepan of boiling water and cook for 8 minutes or until al dente. 2 Drain and set aside. 3 Place the broccoli in a large saucepan of boiling water and cook until tender. Remove broccoli and repeat for the zucchini in fresh water. 4 Drain and allow to cool. 5 Heat the oil in a frying pan over medium heat. Add the onion and garlic, and cook until sizzling. Add the chilli and cook for 1 minute or until softened. 6 Add the pasta and coat well with the oil. Add the broccoli and zucchini and toss together gently. 7 Pour over lemon juice, season with salt and serve immediately.

Serving idea
Serve with parma ham

2 large savoy cabbages
   (about 500 grams each)
2 tablespoons butter
1 leek, finely chopped
2 cloves garlic, minced
⅓ cup cream
sea salt
black pepper
100 grams blue cheese, crumbled
2 cups vegetable stock (recipe, page 152)

1 Chop one of the cabbages into 2 cm cubes and discard the core. 2 Bring a saucepan of water to the boil and cook the chopped cabbage until tender. 3 Drain well, squeezing the cabbage to remove excess water. Set aside. 4 Melt 1 tablespoon of the butter in a frying pan over medium heat. Add the leek and garlic, and cook until softened. 5 Add the cooked cabbage and the cream. Season with salt and pepper to taste. 6 Cover and cook for a further 10 minutes or until the cream has thickened. 7 Remove from the heat and set aside to cool. 8 Preheat the oven to 180°C. 9 Bring a large saucepan of water to the boil and cook the other cabbage for 5–6 minutes. 10 Once cooked, peel 10–12 leaves and place them on a flat, dry surface. 11 Pat with absorbent kitchen paper to remove any excess water. 12 Place a small amount of the cabbage and cream mixture on a leaf, then add a small amount of the crumbled blue cheese. 13 Fold the leaf over, roll it up and secure with string. Repeat for the remaining leaves. 14 Place the parcels in a baking dish, pour over the stock and top with pieces of the remaining tablespoon of butter. 15 Braise for 20 minutes or until just golden.

Cabbage with Tomato
and Parmigiano Reggiano

400 grams cabbage
⅓ cup olive oil
1 large onion, sliced into rings
3 cloves garlic, minced
500 grams tinned tomatoes, chopped
½ cup chicken stock
2 tablespoons red wine vinegar
2 teaspoons thyme, picked
sea salt
black pepper
sugar
25 grams butter
Parmigiano Reggiano cheese, for grating

1 Cut the cabbage into strips and discard the core. 2 Heat the oil in a frying pan over medium heat. Add the onion and garlic, and cook until golden. 3 Add the cabbage and cook for 1 minute. 4 Add the tomatoes, stock, vinegar and thyme. 5 Season to taste with salt, pepper and sugar. 6 Slowly bring to the boil, then cover and simmer for 20−25 minutes or until the cabbage is softened. 7 Remove from the heat and stir in the butter. 8 Place the cabbage mixture in a serving bowl and cover generously with grated cheese.

Serving idea
Serve with grilled Italian sausages

800 grams cabbage, cut into chunks
90 grams butter
4 cloves garlic, minced
2 stalks celery, finely chopped
200 grams dried bread (dry bread in oven
    if necessary), cut into chunks
5 cups chicken stock
sea salt
black pepper
250 grams Taleggio cheese, grated

1 Bring a large pot of water to the boil and cook the cabbage until softened. Drain well and set aside. 2 In a large, heavy based pot, melt the butter over medium heat. Add the garlic and cook until it sizzles. 3 Add the celery and cook for 1 minute or until just tender. 4 Add the cabbage and bread chunks. Stir together. 5 Pour in the stock and season with salt and pepper. 6 Simmer for 15 minutes. 7 Add the Taleggio and simmer for 5 more minutes. 8 Serve immediately.

Serving idea
Serve with garlic toast

Salad of Raw Cabbage
with Soy and Mirin Dressing

⅓ cup grapeseed oil

1 teaspoon sesame oil

¼ cup mirin

2 tablespoons rice wine vinegar

2 teaspoons soy sauce

1 small red chilli, seeded and chopped

1 large cabbage

1 For the dressing, mix together the grapeseed oil, sesame oil, mirin, vinegar, soy sauce and chilli in a bowl. 2 Remove the core from the cabbage and cut the remaining cabbage into thin strips. 3 Pour the sauce over the cabbage and toss well. 4 Serve immediately.

Serving idea

Serve with grilled soy chicken skewers

100 grams rice vermicelli noodles
1 small carrot, julienned
1 small cucumber, julienned
1 cup snow pea sprouts
2 cups shredded cabbage
4 stalks green onion,
    quartered and sliced
½ cup roughly chopped coriander leaves
⅓ cup roughly chopped mint
¼ cup sliced Thai basil
1 clove garlic, minced
2 small red chillies, finely chopped
salt
juice of 2 small limes
12 large Vietnamese rice paper wrappers
12 lettuce leaves, roughly chopped
2 tablespoons sweet chilli sauce
1 tablespoon fish sauce
½ teaspoon caster sugar

1 Soak the noodles in warm water until softened. Drain and set aside. 2 In a large bowl, mix the carrot, cucumber, sprouts, cabbage, green onion, coriander, mint and basil. 3 In a separate bowl, mix the garlic and chilli to form a paste. Add salt to taste. 4 Set aside 2 tablespoons of the lime juice for the dipping sauce. Add the remaining lime juice to the garlic and chilli paste, and combine. 5 Pour this mixture over the vegetables and toss together. 6 Soak three rice papers at a time in warm water until soft. Transfer to a flat, dry surface. 7 Place a small amount of the noodles onto each rice paper and top with some of the vegetable mixture. 8 Add some lettuce. Fold over and roll up to secure. 9 Repeat for the remaining rolls. 10 For the dipping sauce, combine the chilli sauce, fish sauce, sugar and the reserved lime juice.

Serving idea
Serve with grilled prawn skewers

4 large red, green or yellow capsicums
olive oil
sea salt
black pepper

1 Preheat the grill to medium–high.
2 Brush the capsicums with olive oil and place them under the hot grill. Cook until the skins have blistered all over, turning frequently. 3 Remove from the grill and place in a bowl. Cover tightly with cling film. The capsicums will steam and the skins will be easy to remove. 4 Rub the skin from each capsicum, slice in half lengthwise and remove the seeds. 5 If you're not using the roasted capsicum straightaway, slice it into strips and season with salt and pepper. Store covered with a little oil in an airtight container. 6 Refrigerate until ready to use. 7 Serve with olives and drizzled with aged balsamic vinegar.

Serving idea
Serve on an antipasto plate

Roasted Capsicum Halves
with Olives, Capers and Basil

2 large red capsicums, halved and seeded
5 tablespoons olive oil
2 cloves garlic, minced
2 tablespoons salted capers, rinsed
     and chopped
100 grams kalamata olives, pitted
     and chopped
2 small tomatoes, finely chopped
2 tablespoons roughly chopped basil
1 tablespoon roughly chopped flat-leaf parsley
sea salt
black pepper

1 Preheat the oven to 200°C. 2 Place the capsicum halves on an oiled baking tray. 3 Baste capsicums with 2 tablespoons of the oil and roast for 15 minutes. 4 In a bowl, combine the remaining oil, garlic, capers, olives, tomatoes, basil and parsley. 5 Season to taste with salt and pepper. 6 Spoon the olive mixture into each capsicum half, spreading the mixture throughout the cavity to fill evenly. 7 Return to the oven and roast for 20 minutes or until the tops are crisp and the edges of the capsicum are slightly burnt. 8 Serve warm.

Serving idea
Serve with grilled fish

Salad of Roasted Capsicum
and Buffalo Mozzarella

2 large roasted red capsicums
(recipe, page 45)
200 grams buffalo mozzarella
¼ cup roughly chopped flat-leaf parsley
1 tablespoon olive oil
80 grams baby spinach leaves, rinsed
1 bunch rocket leaves, stems removed
sea salt
black pepper

1 Slice the roasted capsicums into thin strips. 2 Cut the mozzarella into small slices and mix with the capsicum. 3 Add the parsley, olive oil, spinach leaves and rocket, and toss together. 4 Season with salt and pepper.

Serving idea
Serve with grilled chicken breast

Spaghetti with Roasted Capsicum, Chilli Oil and Baby Spinach

2 large roasted red capsicums
(recipe, page 45)
500 grams spaghetti
⅓ cup chilli oil (recipe, page 147)
250 grams baby spinach leaves
sea salt
black pepper

1 Slice the roasted capsicums and set aside.
2 Add the spaghetti to a large saucepan of boiling water, and cook for 8 minutes or until al dente. 3 Strain and set aside. 4 Heat a little of the chilli oil in a frying pan over medium heat. Add the capsicum and spaghetti.
5 Gradually pour in enough chilli oil to coat the pasta well. Toss gently. 6 Add the spinach leaves and continue to toss. 7 When the spinach has just started to wilt, remove from the heat and season with salt and pepper.
8 Serve immediately.

Serving idea
Serve with freshly grated pecorino cheese

4 large roasted red capsicums
     (recipe, page 45)
6 large black olives, pitted
2 tablespoons salted capers, rinsed
½ cup basil leaves
2 tablespoons roughly chopped
     flat-leaf parsley
4 tablespoons olive oil
2 teaspoons balsamic vinegar
sea salt
black pepper

1 Slice the roasted capsicum into thin strips.
2 Place the capsicum, olives, capers, basil
and parsley in a food processor or blender,
and mix thoroughly. With the motor still
running, gradually pour in the olive oil and
vinegar, and blend until smooth. 3 If the
mixture is too thick, add more olive oil until
you reach the desired consistency. 4 Season
to taste with salt and pepper.

Serving idea
Serve with barbecued eggplant

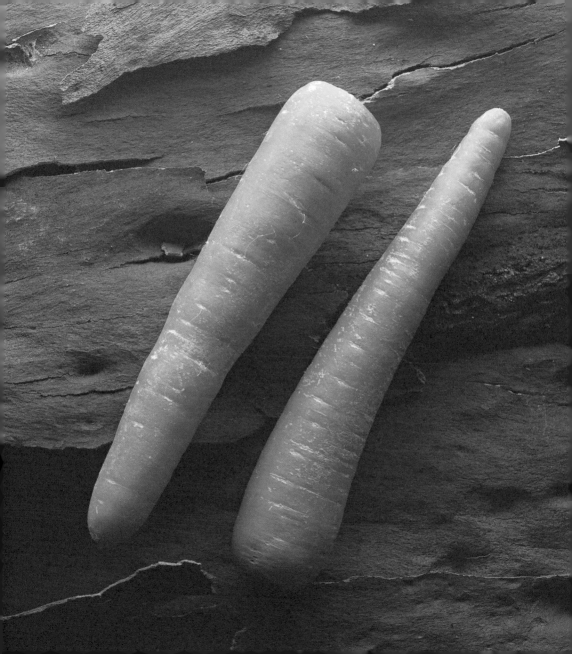

400 grams carrots, peeled and chopped
1 medium potato, peeled and chopped
1 tablespoon ginger, minced
110 grams butter, cut into small cubes
2 sprigs thyme, chopped
sea salt
white pepper

1 Place the carrot and potato in a large saucepan. Fill the pan with just enough water to cover the vegetables. 2 Cover, bring to the boil and simmer for 15 minutes. 3 Add the ginger and cook for 10 minutes or until the vegetables have softened. 4 Drain, and reserve the liquid. 5 Place the vegetables in a food processor or blender and process until smooth. You may need to add some of the reserved liquid if the mixture is too thick. 6 Transfer the mixture to a saucepan. Add the butter and thyme, and cook over a medium heat until the butter has melted. 7 Season to taste with salt and pepper. 8 Serve immediately or cover in oil and store in an airtight container in the refrigerator until ready to use (the purée will keep for 1–2 weeks).

Serving idea
Serve with braised oxtail

Carrots with Spinach, Hijiki and Sesame

1 cup hijiki
2 tablespoons soy sauce
2 tablespoons sesame oil
2 tablespoons minced ginger
3 medium carrots, julienned
1 cup roughly chopped baby spinach leaves
sea salt
2 tablespoons sesame seeds, toasted

1 Soak the hijiki in water for 15 minutes. Drain well. 2 Place the hijiki and soy sauce in a saucepan, cover with water and slowly bring to the boil. Simmer for 10 minutes. 3 Drain and set aside. 4 Heat the oil in a frying pan over medium heat. Add the ginger and carrot, and cook for 2 minutes or until just golden. 5 Add the hijiki and cook for 4–5 minutes. 6 Add the spinach and toss together for 30 seconds. 7 Remove from the heat, season to taste with salt and toss through the sesame seeds. 8 Serve immediately.

Serving idea
Serve with steamed white fish

½ cup roughly chopped coriander leaves
2 cloves garlic
80 grams blanched almonds, roughly chopped
100 grams Parmesan cheese, grated
½ cup grapeseed oil
sea salt
white pepper

500 grams baby carrots, trimmed and peeled
4 tablespoons olive oil

1 To prepare the pesto, place the coriander, garlic, almonds and cheese in a food processor and blend to a paste. With the motor still running, gradually pour in the grapeseed oil and process until smooth.
2 Season to taste with salt and pepper.
3 Pour the pesto into a jar and set aside until ready to use. 4 Preheat the oven to 200°C. 5 Slice the carrots lengthwise and place in a baking dish. 6 Add the olive oil, coating the carrot well, and season with salt and pepper. Add a little water, cover with foil and roast for 20–25 minutes or until tender. 7 Remove the foil, toss the carrots in the oil and cook for a further 5–10 minutes or until the carrots are slightly browned. 8 Serve with the pesto tossed through the carrots.

Serving idea
Serve with rare roast beef

1 cup plain flour
1 teaspoon baking powder
1 pinch salt
½ teaspoon turmeric
½ cup milk
2 large eggs, beaten
2 small red chillies, seeded and chopped
2 cups finely chopped cauliflower
¼ cup finely chopped coriander
4 tablespoons vegetable oil

1 In a large mixing bowl, combine the flour, baking powder, salt and turmeric. In another bowl, combine the milk and eggs. 2 Slowly pour the liquid into the flour mixture, whisking until smooth. 3 Add the chilli, cauliflower and coriander, and combine well. 4 Roll a small amount of the mixture between your hands to make a ball, then flatten into a patty. 5 Repeat for the remainder of the mixture, setting the patties aside on a floured, flat surface. 6 Heat the oil in a frying pan over medium heat. Add the fritters and cook for 2–3 minutes each side or until the fritters have turned golden. 7 Serve immediately.

Serving idea
Serve with ham, tomato and mozzarella salad

1 head cauliflower (about 500 grams),
    cut into florets
2 tablespoons butter
1 small onion, finely chopped
½ stalk celery, finely chopped
1 tablespoon chopped oregano
2½ tablespoons plain flour
2 cups milk
1 bay leaf, cut in half
sea salt
white pepper
185 grams Gruyère cheese, finely grated
3 tablespoons breadcrumbs

1 Preheat the oven to 180°C. 2 Add the cauliflower to a large saucepan of boiling water and cook for 5 minutes or until just tender. 3 Drain and set aside. 4 Melt the butter in a heavy based saucepan over medium heat. Add the onion, celery and oregano, and cook until softened. 5 Stir in the flour and cook for 5 minutes or until smooth. 6 Pour in half the milk and bring to a simmer, stirring constantly. When the milk has reached a boil and the consistency is smooth, add the remaining milk and the bay leaf. 7 Simmer gently for a further 5–10 minutes until the sauce is smooth. 8 Season to taste with salt and pepper, and remove the bay leaf. 9 Stir in two-thirds of the cheese and remove from the heat. 10 Place the cauliflower in a buttered gratin dish or a baking dish large enough to hold it in a single layer. 11 Ladle over the sauce and sprinkle with the remaining cheese. 12 Top with breadcrumbs and bake for 20–25 minutes or until the gratin is bubbling and slightly browned on top. 13 Serve immediately.

Serving idea
Serve with any game roast, such as duck

Steamed Cauliflower and Beans
with Chilli and Garlic Dressing

2 large red chillies, seeded and sliced
1 clove garlic, minced
1 tablespoon lime juice
⅓ cup olive oil
1 teaspoon brown sugar or to taste
sea salt
black pepper

250 grams beans, trimmed
500 grams cauliflower, cut into florets

1 To prepare the dressing, combine the chilli, garlic, lime juice, olive oil and brown sugar in a mixing bowl. Season to taste with salt and pepper, and more sugar if necessary. Set aside. 2 Bring a large saucepan or pot of water to the boil. Cover with a bamboo steaming basket. 3 Place the beans in the basket and steam for 3–4 minutes. Add the cauliflower and steam for a further 5 minutes or until just tender. 4 Pour the dressing over the vegetables and toss gently. 5 Serve warm.

Serving idea
Serve with ham off the bone

Stir-fried Cauliflower with Ginger, Lemon and Coriander

⅓ cup olive oil plus extra for serving
3 cloves garlic
1 tablespoon ginger, minced
800 grams cauliflower, cut into florets
sea salt
black pepper
1 small lemon, juiced
⅓ cup roughly chopped coriander leaves

1 Heat the oil in a large frying pan or wok over medium heat. Add the garlic and ginger, and cook until sizzling. Add the cauliflower and toss to coat well with the oil. Season to taste with salt. 2 Stir-fry for 2–3 minutes. Add a little water, cover and simmer for a further 2 minutes or until just tender. The cauliflower should still be crisp. 3 Remove from the heat and drain any excess liquid. 4 Season generously with pepper, pour over the lemon juice and sprinkle with coriander. 5 Toss together gently. 6 To serve, drizzle with a little extra olive oil.

Serving idea
Serve with steamed white fish

Yellow Curry of Cauliflower and Snow Peas

2 tablespoons vegetable oil
1 small onion, finely chopped
1 tablespoon minced ginger
2 tablespoons yellow curry paste
400 ml coconut milk
1 cup vegetable stock (recipe, page 152)
2 tablespoons caster sugar
3 stalks lemongrass, cut into 4 cm lengths
3 lime leaves, cut into thin strips
1 teaspoon turmeric
1 teaspoon garam masala
800 grams cauliflower, cut into florets
500 grams snow peas, strings removed
juice of 1 small lime
1 bunch coriander, roughly chopped

1 Heat the oil in a heavy based casserole or saucepan over medium–high heat. 2 Add the onion and ginger, and sauté until softened. Add the curry paste and sauté for 4–5 minutes or until fragrant. 3 Pour in the coconut milk and stir well. Add the vegetable stock, caster sugar, lemongrass, lime leaves, turmeric and garam masala. 4 Slowly bring to the boil, stirring frequently until combined. 5 Add the cauliflower and simmer for 6–8 minutes or until the cauliflower is tender. 6 Reduce the heat and add the snow peas. Simmer for 2 minutes or until snow peas are just tender. 7 Remove from the heat. Stir in the lime juice and sprinkle over the coriander. 8 Serve immediately.

Serving idea
Serve with steamed basmati rice

Celery and Apple Salad
with Creamy Mayo

2 large egg yolks
1 large egg
2 teaspoons Dijon mustard
1 tablespoon lemon juice
salt
white pepper
1½ cups grapeseed oil
2 tablespoons finely chopped parsley

8 medium celery stalks, trimmed
2 small apples
⅓ cup walnuts, toasted and chopped

1 To prepare the mayonnaise, place the egg yolks, egg, mustard, lemon juice, salt and pepper in a food processor. Process for 1 minute. 2 With the motor running, gradually pour in the oil and continue to process until thickened. Adjust seasoning if necessary. 3 Pour the mayonnaise into a container. Stir in the parsley and refrigerate until ready to use. 4 Cut the celery into quarters crosswise and then into thin strips. 5 Peel the apple and cut into thin slices. 6 Combine the celery, apple and walnuts, and spoon the mayonnaise over the mixture. 7 Toss together and serve immediately.

Serving idea
Serve with roasted quail

4 large corn cobs
3 medium tomatoes, peeled and chopped
sea salt
1 small onion, finely chopped
1 clove garlic, minced
1 small red chilli, seeded and chopped
⅓ cup roughly chopped coriander leaves
juice of 1 small lime
olive oil for drizzling
1 large avocado, peeled and chopped

1 Bring a large saucepan of water to the boil, add the corn and cook until a kernel can be easily removed with a knife. Allow to cool, then remove all the kernels with a knife.
2 In a large mixing bowl, place the corn, tomato, salt, onion, garlic, chilli, coriander and lime juice. 3 Toss together and drizzle with olive oil. 4 Just before serving, toss through the avocado.

Serving idea
Serve with fresh prawns

8 large Roma tomatoes, chopped

1 medium red capsicum, seeded and chopped

2 cloves garlic, chopped

8 medium cucumbers, peeled and chopped

2 cups tomato juice

½ cup red wine vinegar

1 pinch cayenne pepper

sea salt

black pepper

½ cup extra virgin olive oil

½ cup chopped dill

1 Put the tomato, capsicum, garlic and half the cucumber in a food processor, and process until smooth. 2 Pour into a bowl and stir in the tomato juice, vinegar, cayenne, salt and pepper. Refrigerate until ready to serve. 3 To serve, stir in the olive oil and remaining cucumber. Adjust seasoning to taste. 4 Garnish with the chopped dill.

Serving idea

Serve with sourdough bread

Cucumber, Pear and Rocket Salad with Goat's Cheese

4 medium cucumbers, peeled and sliced
2 large pears, peeled and sliced
1 bunch rocket, stems removed
1 tablespoon lemon juice
4 tablespoons grapeseed oil
1 teaspoon sansho powder
sea salt
100 grams goat's cheese, sliced

1 In a large bowl, gently toss the cucumber, pear, rocket, lemon juice and grapeseed oil. 2 Sprinkle with sansho powder and season to taste with salt. 3 To serve, garnish with goat's cheese slices.

Serving idea
Serve with poached salmon

4 large cucumbers, peeled
1 tablespoon sugar
3 tablespoons rice wine vinegar
3 tablespoons vegetable oil
3 small red chillies, seeded and chopped
1 tablespoon fish sauce
½ cup chopped Vietnamese mint
2 spring onions, finely sliced
⅓ cup peanuts, roasted and chopped
3 tablespoons chopped coriander

1 Cut the cucumbers in half lengthwise and spoon out the seeds. Cut into 1 cm lengths. 2 In a small bowl, dissolve the sugar in the vinegar. 3 Add the vegetable oil, chilli and fish sauce, and stir to combine. 4 Stir in the mint and spring onion. 5 Pour the dressing over the cucumber, and garnish with the peanuts and coriander.

Serving idea
Serve with steamed white fish

3 medium eggplants
3 cloves garlic, minced
sea salt
¼ cup tahini
juice of 1 small lemon
¼ cup finely chopped mint leaves
1 pinch cumin
black pepper
3 tablespoons extra virgin olive oil

1 Roast the eggplants over a barbecue grill, turning frequently until the skin has blackened. Set aside to cool. 2 Remove the skin from the eggplants, then rinse each eggplant quickly. 3 Press each eggplant with absorbent kitchen paper to release the bitter juices. 4 Place the eggplant, garlic, salt, tahini, lemon juice, mint, cumin and a generous grind of pepper in a food processor and blend until smooth.
5 Transfer the eggplant mixture to a bowl. Stir in the olive oil until blended, and serve.

Serving idea
Serve with lamb racks

2 large eggplants

sea salt, for sprinkling and seasoning

1 kilogram ripe tomatoes, chopped

½ cup roughly chopped basil

black pepper

2 tablespoons extra virgin olive oil plus
    extra for brushing

150 grams mozzarella cheese, thinly sliced

60 grams Parmesan cheese, grated

1 Preheat the oven to 180°C. 2 Slice the eggplant into rounds about 1 cm thick. Sprinkle with salt and let stand for 1 hour. 3 Meanwhile, place the tomatoes and half (¼ cup) of the basil in a large, heavy based saucepan. Cook for 10 minutes or until the tomatoes have softened. 4 Remove from the heat. Pass the tomatoes through a food mill or process in a blender and return to the pan. 5 Season to taste with salt and pepper. Stir in the olive oil and set aside. 6 Brush each eggplant round with olive oil and place in a frying pan over medium heat. 7 Fry the eggplant in batches for 4–5 minutes or until slightly browned on both sides. 8 In a baking dish large enough to hold the eggplant in two layers, cover the bottom with about a third of the tomato sauce. 9 Add half the eggplant in overlapping slices and top with mozzarella. Sprinkle with the Parmesan and remaining basil. 10 Lay the other eggplant slices on top, and cover with the remaining tomato sauce. 11 Season generously with pepper, place in the oven and bake for 30 minutes or until bubbling.

Serving idea

Serve with pasta and garlic oil

3 medium eggplants, sliced

olive oil

sea salt

black pepper

200 grams haloumi, sliced

6 small Roma tomatoes, quartered

juice of 1 small lemon

⅓ cup chopped parsley

1 Brush the eggplant slices with a little olive oil and place in a frying pan or on a barbecue grill. Cook for 2–3 minutes each side or until charred and golden. 2 Set aside on absorbent kitchen paper (to absorb any excess oil). Season with salt and pepper. 3 Brush the haloumi slices with a little olive oil, place on the hot grill and cook for 1 minute on each side. 4 Transfer to a bowl and toss with the tomatoes, lemon juice and parsley. 5 To serve, place the grilled eggplant on a serving plate and top with the haloumi and tomato. Drizzle with olive oil.

Serving idea

Serve with barbecued tuna steaks

3 tablespoons miso
2 tablespoons rice wine vinegar
2 tablespoons mirin
¼ teaspoon sesame oil

8 Japanese eggplants
3 tablespoons olive oil
sea salt
1 teaspoon black sesame seeds

1 In a small bowl, combine the miso, vinegar, mirin and sesame oil. Set aside. 2 Cut the eggplants lengthwise into slices 1 cm thick. 3 Heat the oil in a frying pan over medium heat. Cook the eggplant for 1–2 minutes on each side or until golden. 4 Transfer to a plate and season to taste with salt. 5 Arrange the eggplant slices on a serving plate. Spoon over the miso sauce and sprinkle with sesame seeds.

Serving idea
Serve with spinach salad

2 large eggplants
sea salt
½ cup olive oil
pepper
1 small onion, finely chopped
2 cloves garlic, finely chopped
1 small red chilli, seeded and chopped
juice and grated zest of 1 large lemon
1 tablespoon rice wine vinegar
1 small tomato, diced
½ cup roughly chopped basil leaves

1 Cut the eggplant into 2 cm cubes. Season with salt and set aside for 30 minutes. 2 Pat the eggplant dry with absorbent kitchen paper. 3 Heat the oil in a frying pan over medium–high heat. When the oil is nearly smoking, add the eggplant and toss well in the olive oil. Reduce the heat and sauté for about 10 minutes or until golden. 4 Season to taste with salt and pepper. 5 Transfer the eggplant to a bowl and set aside. 6 Return the frying pan to a medium heat with a little more oil. Add the onion, garlic and chilli, and sauté until golden. Add the lemon juice, lemon zest, vinegar and tomato, and cook for 1 minute. 7 Add the onion and garlic mixture to the eggplant and toss with the basil. 8 Serve immediately.

Serving idea
Serve with spaghetti

2 medium fennel bulbs, trimmed and outer
   leaves removed
2 medium oranges, peeled
4 tablespoons orange juice
1 tablespoon lemon juice
1 teaspoon sugar
2 tablespoons olive oil
sea salt
black pepper

1 Slice the fennel bulbs crosswise into paper-thin rounds. 2 Cut the oranges into thin segments. 3 Place the fennel and orange into a large bowl and toss together. 4 In a separate bowl, stir the orange juice, lemon juice and sugar until the sugar dissolves. 5 Add the oil, salt and pepper, and stir until combined. 6 Pour the dressing over the fennel and orange, and refrigerate until ready to serve.

Serving idea
Serve with chicken tagine

4 cups chicken or vegetable stock
    (recipe, page 152)
1 cup dry white wine
2 tablespoons olive oil
2 tablespoons butter, chopped,
    plus 1 tablespoon for sautéing
1 small onion, finely chopped
2 cloves garlic, minced
3 small fennel bulbs, cut into large chunks
juice of ½ small lemon
2 cups arborio rice
60 grams Parmesan cheese, grated
1 bunch rocket leaves, stems removed
salt
pepper

1 Place the stock and wine in a large saucepan and bring to a simmer. 2 Heat the oil and 1 tablespoon of the butter in a large, heavy based saucepan. Add the onion and garlic, and sauté until golden. 3 Add the fennel and lemon juice, and cook for 5 minutes or until tender. 4 Remove the fennel and set aside. 5 Add the rice and coat well in the oil. Cook until the rice is translucent. 6 Add 1 cup of the stock, stirring continuously until the stock has been absorbed. 7 Continue adding the stock 1 cup at a time until the rice is soft and the consistency is creamy. 8 Return the fennel to the risotto and toss through. 9 When the risotto is almost cooked, stir through the chopped butter, Parmesan and rocket. 10 Season to taste with salt and black pepper.

Serving idea
Serve with barbecued scallops

2 medium fennel bulbs, trimmed and outer
   leaves removed
2 bunches watercress
125 grams goat's cheese, crumbled
¼ cup extra virgin olive oil
1 tablespoon walnut oil
1 tablespoon sherry vinegar
sea salt
black pepper
1 tablespoon chopped walnuts

1 Slice the fennel crosswise into paper-thin slices. 2 Place the fennel and watercress in a large bowl. Sprinkle over the goat's cheese and toss together. 3 Add the olive oil, walnut oil and vinegar, and season to taste with salt and pepper. 4 Sprinkle over the chopped walnuts, toss together and serve.

Serving idea
Serve with roasted snapper

1 large egg yolk, at room temperature

1 teaspoon Dijon mustard

juice of ½ medium lemon

sea salt

white pepper

¾ cup olive oil

1 large pinch saffron, soaked in
   2 tablespoons warm water

3 medium fennel bulbs, trimmed

2 large eggs, beaten

2 tablespoons milk

¼ cup plain flour

1 cup fine dry breadcrumbs

olive oil for frying

black pepper

1 For the mayonnaise, place the egg yolk, mustard, lemon juice, salt and pepper in a food processor and process until smooth. With the motor running, gradually pour in the olive oil and blend until thickened. 2 Remove to a bowl and stir in the saffron and its soaking liquid. Set aside. 3 Cut the fennel into 2 cm wedges. 4 Blanch the fennel in a large saucepan of boiling water for 8–10 minutes or until just tender. 5 Remove from the heat and drain thoroughly. 6 In a bowl, combine the beaten eggs and milk. 7 Roll the pieces of fennel in the flour to coat lightly. 8 Dip the fennel into the egg mixture, then the breadcrumbs. 9 Heat the olive oil in a frying pan over medium–high heat. Add the fennel and cook until all the sides are golden. 10 Remove from the heat and season with salt and pepper. 11 To serve, arrange the fennel pieces on a platter with the saffron mayonnaise to the side.

Serving idea

Serve with poached trout

2 large fennel bulbs, trimmed and outer
    leaves removed
1 cup vegetable stock (recipe, page 152)
1 medium lemon, cut into eighths
4 cloves garlic, sliced
10 large kalamata olives
sea salt
white pepper
olive oil

1 Preheat the oven to 220°C. 2 Cut the fennel
lengthwise into thick slices. 3 Place the
slices in a roasting pan large enough to hold
them in a single layer. Pour over the stock.
4 Place the lemon chunks, garlic and olives
between the fennel pieces. 5 Season with
salt and pepper, and drizzle with a little
olive oil. 6 Roast the fennel for 15 minutes.
Remove briefly from the oven and turn the
fennel slices over. 7 Season with salt and
pepper again, and drizzle with a little more
olive oil. 8 Roast for a further 15 minutes or
until the fennel is tender and the edges have
started to brown.

Serving idea
**Serve with pasta, garnished
with Parmesan**

75 grams butter, chopped, plus 50 grams
   for the mustard cream
2 tablespoons olive oil
8 medium leeks, trimmed and washed
2 cups chicken or vegetable stock
   (recipe, page 152)
2 medium golden shallots, finely chopped
1 cup dry white wine
2 cups thickened cream
2 tablespoons Dijon mustard
1 small bunch chives, finely chopped
sea salt
white pepper

1 Preheat the oven to 200°C. 2 Spread the chopped butter and the oil over the base of a roasting pan large enough to hold the leeks in one layer. 3 Add the leeks and roast for 10 minutes. 4 Remove from the oven and turn the leeks over. Roast for a further 10 minutes. 5 Remove from the oven again and add the stock. 6 Roast for another 10 minutes or until the leeks have started to brown slightly and the liquid has reduced. 7 Set aside. 8 For the mustard cream, melt the remaining 50 grams of butter in a small saucepan over medium heat. Add the shallots and sauté for 5 minutes or until softened. 9 Increase the heat a little, add the wine and slowly bring to the boil. Simmer until the liquid has reduced by half. 10 Stir in the cream and simmer gently until the sauce has thickened slightly. Stir in the mustard. 11 Add half the chives and season to taste with salt and pepper. 12 Arrange the leeks on a serving platter, drizzle over the mustard cream and garnish with the remaining chives.

Serving idea
Serve with braised chicken

2 medium fennel bulbs, trimmed and outer
     leaves removed
2 large leeks, trimmed of roots and
     dark leaves
3 tablespoons butter
3 cloves garlic, minced
1 large potato, peeled and chopped
1 litre chicken or vegetable stock
     (recipe, page 152)
sea salt
white pepper
juice of ½ small lemon
2 tablespoons Pernod
½ cup thickened cream, or to taste

1 Cut the fennel bulbs and leeks into thin slices. 2 Wash well and set aside to drain. 3 Melt the butter in a large, heavy based saucepan or pot over medium heat. Add the garlic and cook until softened. 4 Add the fennel and leeks, and cook for 10 minutes or until softened. 5 Add the potato and stock. Season with salt and pepper. 6 Cover and simmer for 30 minutes or until vegetables are soft. 7 Remove from the heat and allow to cool. 8 Pour the soup into a food processor or blender and blend until smooth. 9 Return the soup to the pot and bring to a slow simmer. 10 Add the lemon juice and Pernod. Adjust seasonings to taste. 11 Add the cream and stir to combine. 12 Remove from the heat and serve immediately.

Serving idea
Serve with Parmesan and bread

3 tablespoons butter

2 tablespoons olive oil

6 medium leeks, sliced

¼ cup chopped parsley

250 grams ready-made puff pastry

150 grams goat's cheese

black pepper

1 Preheat the oven to 200°C. 2 Melt the butter and oil in a frying pan over medium heat. Add the leek and sauté for 10 minutes or until the leek has softened. 3 Add the parsley and cook for 2 minutes. 4 Remove from the heat and set aside to cool. 5 On a flat surface, lightly dusted with flour, roll out the pastry until about 4–5 mm thick. 6 Cut a rectangle measuring approximately 20 cm x 26 cm. 7 Place the rectangle on a baking tray and prick with a fork. Part bake for 10 minutes. 8 Remove from the oven and spread over the goat's cheese. Top with the leek mixture and season with black pepper. 9 Bake in the oven for a further 10–12 minutes or until the pastry is golden. 10 Serve immediately.

Serving idea

Serve with watercress salad

75 grams butter plus 35 grams for
   the croutons
1 large onion, finely chopped
2 cloves garlic, minced
1 stalk celery, finely chopped
8 large leeks, finely sliced
6 medium potatoes, peeled and thinly sliced
4 sprigs thyme
sea salt
black pepper
60 grams Gruyère cheese, grated
1 teaspoon Dijon mustard
8 slices French bread

1 Melt 75 grams of butter in a large saucepan or pot over medium heat. 2 Add the onion, garlic, celery, leek and potato. Cover and cook for 10 minutes or until the leek has softened. 3 Add just enough water to cover the vegetables. Add the thyme and season with salt and pepper. 4 Simmer for 10 minutes or until the potato is tender. 5 Remove the thyme sprigs and discard. 6 Allow the vegetable mixture to cool slightly before transferring to a food processor or blender. Process until smooth. 7 Return the soup to the saucepan, and adjust seasonings to taste. Set aside. 8 Preheat the grill to high. 9 Mix the cheese, mustard and remaining butter in a small bowl. Season with a grind of black pepper. 10 For the croutons, toast the bread on both sides and then spread a little of the cheese mixture on each slice. Grill until the cheese begins to bubble and melt. 11 Return the soup to the heat and bring to the boil. 12 Ladle the soup into bowls and serve the croutons on the side.

Serving idea
Serve with crusty sourdough bread

Poached Leeks with
Green Peppercorn Sauce

12 large leeks, trimmed and hard outer
    leaves removed

2 egg yolks, beaten
200 ml sour cream
2 teaspoons Dijon mustard
50 grams butter
2 tablespoons lemon juice
2 tablespoons green peppercorns
sea salt
black pepper

1 Soak the leeks in cold water and rinse well. 2 Add the leeks to a large pot of boiling water. Simmer for 10 minutes or until tender but still firm. 3 Drain and set aside. 4 In a small bowl, combine the egg yolks, sour cream and mustard. 5 Melt the butter in a frying pan over medium heat. Add the lemon juice and peppercorns, and cook for 1–2 minutes. 6 Reduce the heat to low. Stir in the egg yolk mixture until thoroughly combined and the sauce starts to thicken. 7 Season to taste with salt and pepper. 8 To serve, arrange the leeks on a platter and drizzle over the peppercorn sauce.

Serving idea
Serve with pan-fried chicken breasts

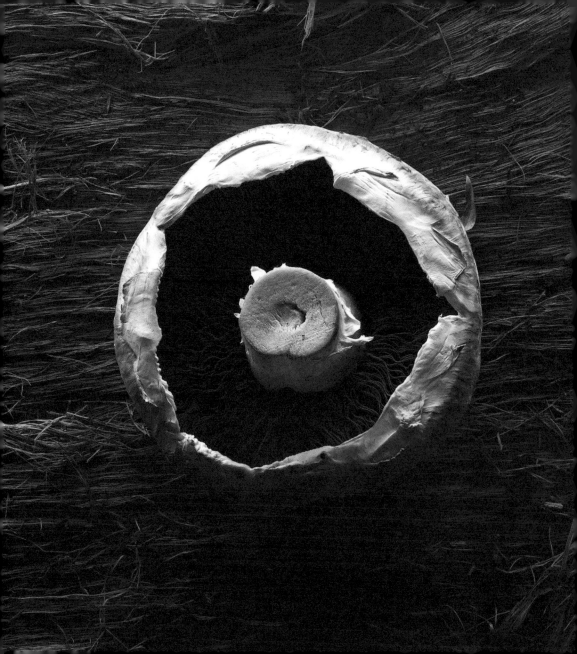

5 cups chicken or vegetable stock
   (recipe, page 152)
1 cup dry white wine
1 tablespoon olive oil
3 tablespoons butter
1 small onion, finely chopped
2 cloves garlic, minced
500 grams fresh mushrooms, thickly sliced
2 cups arborio rice
½ cup chopped parsley
60 grams Taleggio cheese, grated
salt
black pepper

1 Place the stock and wine in a large saucepan and bring to a simmer. 2 Heat the oil and 2 tablespoons of the butter in a large, heavy based saucepan over medium heat. Add the onion and garlic and sauté until golden. 3 Add the mushroom and sauté until tender. 4 Remove the mushroom and set aside. 5 Add the rice and coat well in the oils. Cook until the rice is translucent. 6 Add 1 cup of stock, stirring continuously until it has been absorbed. 7 Continue adding the stock 1 cup at a time until the rice is soft and the consistency is creamy. 8 Add the mushroom and parsley and stir through. 9 When the risotto is almost cooked, stir through the remaining butter and Taleggio. 10 Season with salt and pepper.

Serving idea
Serve with prosciutto

Miso Soup with Udon Noodles
and Shiitake Mushrooms

1 litre water
1 x 6 cm piece konbu
1 cup bonito flakes
4 tablespoons red miso paste
250 grams dried udon noodles
1 small red chilli, seeded and sliced
8 medium shiitake mushrooms
1 cup roughly chopped spinach leaves

1 Place the water and konbu in a saucepan and slowly bring to a simmer. 2 Remove the konbu and add the bonito flakes. Slowly bring to the boil. 3 Once the liquid begins to boil, remove from the heat and set aside for 5 minutes. 4 Strain the liquid through a fine-meshed sieve into a saucepan. 5 Mix the miso paste with a little water so it has a runny consistency. 6 Stir in the miso paste, then add the noodles, chilli and mushrooms. Boil for 6–8 minutes or until the noodles are al dente. 7 Stir the spinach through and remove from the heat. 8 Ladle into individual bowls and serve.

Serving idea
Serve with grilled salmon

6 medium artichokes
lemon juice
2 tablespoons butter
1 tablespoon olive oil
2 medium onions, sliced
2 cloves garlic
6 large mushrooms, sliced
8 large eggs
¾ cup cream
sea salt
black pepper
60 grams Parmesan cheese, grated
2 tablespoons roughly chopped parsley

1 **Trim the stems and tops from each artichoke and remove the dark outer leaves. 2 Bring a saucepan of water to the boil. Add the artichokes and simmer for 3–4 minutes or until tender. Drain well. 3 Squeeze a little lemon juice over the artichokes and set aside. 4 Melt the butter and oil in a non-stick frying pan over medium heat. 5 Add the onion and garlic, and sauté for 5 minutes or until soft and golden. 6 Add the mushroom and sauté for 2–3 minutes or until soft. 7 Add the artichokes and toss to combine. 8 Preheat the grill to medium–high. 9 In a bowl, whisk the eggs, cream, salt and pepper. 10 Pour the egg mixture over the mushroom and artichokes. Sprinkle with Parmesan and parsley. 11 Cook the frittata over medium heat for 6–8 minutes or until the eggs have nearly set. The top will still be slightly wet. 12 Place the frittata under the hot grill for 1–2 minutes or until the top is sizzling.**

Serving idea
Serve with roasted capsicum and zucchini recipe for Roasted Capsicum, page 45

2 cups plain flour plus extra for kneading
1 teaspoon active dry yeast
½ teaspoon salt
¾ cup warm water
2 tablespoons olive oil plus extra for oiling
    and drizzling
300 grams Taleggio cheese, sliced
8 large fresh mushrooms, thinly sliced
2 small onions, thinly sliced
¼ cup roughly chopped parsley leaves
sea salt
black pepper

1 Preheat the oven to 180°C. 2 Place the flour, yeast and salt in a large mixing bowl. Stir in the warm water and oil and combine to form a smooth dough. 3 Knead the dough on a lightly floured flat surface for 5 minutes or until the dough is smooth and elastic. You may need to add more flour if the mixture is too sticky. 4 Place the dough in a large, lightly oiled bowl. Cover with cling film and set aside in a warm place for 25 minutes or until the dough has doubled in size. 5 Place the dough on a baking sheet or lightly oiled pizza tray. Knead into a rectangular or round shape. 6 Cover with the Taleggio, mushroom and onion. 7 Drizzle with a little olive oil, top with the parsley, and season with salt and pepper. 8 Place in the oven and cook for 20 minutes or until the pizza dough is golden.

Serving idea
Serve with Rocket and Tomato Salad with Toasted Breadcrumbs
recipe, page 117

4 large field mushrooms, stems removed
6 cloves garlic, roughly chopped
1 cup olive oil
sea salt
black pepper
1 bunch thyme, roughly chopped

1 Preheat the oven to 200°C. 2 Cut the stems off the flat mushroom caps and discard. 3 Place the garlic and 4 tablespoons of the oil in a food processor or blender and process until smooth. 4 Add the remaining oil plus salt and pepper to taste, and process until smooth. 5 Place the mushrooms in a large roasting dish and brush the garlic oil mixture over each mushroom. 6 Set aside to marinate in the oil for ½–3 hours. Turn occasionally. 7 When ready to cook, place the mushrooms in the oven and roast for 8–10 minutes. 8 Remove from the oven briefly and turn the mushrooms over. Sprinkle with the thyme and roast for a further 6 minutes. 9 Serve immediately.

Serving idea
**Serve for breakfast
with grilled Taleggio on toast**

Baked Onions filled with Goat's Cheese and Olives

4 medium brown onions, trimmed and peeled
olive oil
100 grams goat's cheese, crumbled
2 tablespoons fresh breadcrumbs
12 medium kalamata olives,
    pitted and chopped
1 tablespoon finely chopped rosemary

1 Preheat the oven to 180°C. 2 Bring a saucepan of water to the boil. Add the onions and cook for 10 minutes or until just tender. 3 Remove the onions, drain and set aside to cool. 4 When cool, scoop out the centre of each onion, leaving 2–3 outer rings or a 6 mm outer shell. 5 Finely chop the inner sections and set aside. 6 In a mixing bowl, combine the goat's cheese, breadcrumbs, olives, rosemary and chopped onion. Season with salt and pepper. 7 Spoon the mixture into the onion shells and place into an oiled baking dish. 8 Drizzle with a little olive oil. Cover with aluminium foil and bake for 30 minutes. 9 Remove the foil and bake for a further 10 minutes or until golden.

Serving idea
Serve with roast pork chops

1 tablespoon olive oil

6 tablespoons butter

10 large brown onions, peeled and sliced

1 teaspoon sugar

sea salt

1 litre chicken or vegetable
    (recipe, page 152)

2 cups dry white wine

black pepper

4 slices French bread

120 grams Gruyère cheese, finely grated

1 Preheat the oven to 220°C. 2 Melt the oil and 4 tablespoons of the butter in a large, heavy based pot over medium heat. Add the onion, cover and cook for 15–20 minutes or until softened. 3 Add the sugar and season with salt. 4 Increase the heat slightly and sauté uncovered for 5 minutes or until golden. 5 Slowly add the stock and wine and simmer for 25 minutes. Season to taste with salt and pepper. 6 Butter the bread slices on both sides with the remaining butter and place in the oven. Roast until golden brown on both sides. 7 Place a slice of toast in each serving bowl and ladle over the soup. Sprinkle over the grated cheese. 8 Place the bowls in baking trays and bake for 5 minutes in the hot oven or until the cheese has browned slightly. 9 Serve immediately.

Serving idea

Serve with roasted winter vegetables

2 teaspoons active dry yeast
½ teaspoon sugar
½ cup warm water
¼ cup plus 3 tablespoons olive oil
1 large egg, lightly beaten
1 pinch salt
1⅓ cups plain flour
6 large onions, sliced
sea salt
black pepper
3 tablespoons black olive paste
2 sprigs rosemary

1 Place a large baking tray in the oven, and preheat to 220°C. 2 Place the yeast, sugar and water in a bowl and let stand until the mixture bubbles. 3 Add 3 tablespoons of the oil, egg and salt. Stir in the flour until the mixture is smooth. 4 Knead the dough on a lightly floured flat surface for 5 minutes or until the dough is smooth and elastic. You may need to add more flour if the mixture is too sticky. 5 Place the dough in a lightly oiled bowl. Cover with cling film and set aside in a warm place for 30 minutes or until the dough has doubled in size. 6 Place the dough on a lightly floured baking sheet and roll it out into a thin rectangle. Cover with a damp cloth for 30 minutes. 7 Meanwhile, heat the remaining oil in a frying pan over medium heat. Add the onion and season to taste with salt and pepper. 8 Cover and sauté the onion for 35–40 minutes or until it has caramelised. 9 Remove the damp cloth from the dough and cover it with a thin layer of olive paste. 10 Add the onion and rosemary, and season with more pepper. 11 Place the tart on the hot baking tray and bake for 15 minutes or until the crust has browned slightly. 12 Serve immediately.

Serving idea
Serve with a seasonal green salad

Honeyed Parsnip and Carrot with Garlic

250 grams parsnips, trimmed and peeled
250 grams carrots, trimmed and peeled
2 tablespoons butter
1 tablespoon honey
2 teaspoons wholegrain mustard
sea salt
black pepper
½ cup roughly chopped parsley

1 Slice the parsnips and carrots into 5 cm lengths. Cut the thicker ends in half lengthwise so that they will cook evenly. 2 Add the parsnip and carrot to a saucepan of salted boiling water and cook until just tender. 3 Drain and set aside. 4 Melt the butter in a frying pan over medium heat. Add the honey and mustard, and stir together until combined. 5 Add the carrot and parsnip, and cook for 4–5 minutes or until the vegetables are well coated and bubbling. 6 Season to taste with salt and pepper. Toss in the parsley and serve immediately.

Serving idea
Serve with roast chicken

1 teaspoon coriander seeds

1 clove

1 teaspoon cumin seeds

½ teaspoon chilli powder

½ teaspoon allspice

½ teaspoon cardamom seeds

½ teaspoon paprika

1 pinch saffron

3 tablespoons olive oil

2 large onions, peeled and chopped

2 cloves garlic, minced

3 large parsnips, peeled and chopped

2 large carrots, peeled and chopped

2 large potatoes, peeled and chopped

1 litre chicken or vegetable stock
    (recipe, page 152)

1 x 440 gram tin tomatoes,
    drained and chopped

4 dates, pitted and roughly chopped

1 x 440 gram tin of chick peas, drained

1 bunch coriander, roughly chopped

1 Combine the coriander seeds, clove, cumin, chilli, allspice, cardamom, paprika, and saffron, and pound in a mortar until well ground. 2 Heat the olive oil in a large, heavy based casserole or pot over medium heat. 3 Add the onion and garlic, and sauté until softened. Add the spice mixture, stir together and sauté for 3 minutes. 4 Add the parsnip, carrot and potato. Toss well in the spices and sauté for 5 minutes. 5 Add the stock, tomatoes and dates, and simmer for 15–20 minutes or until the vegetables are just tender. 6 Add the chick peas and simmer for a further 5 minutes. If stew is too thick add a little water. 7 Adjust seasonings to taste. 8 Sprinkle with the coriander leaves and serve immediately.

Serving idea

Serve with couscous and yoghurt sauce

1 tablespoon coriander seeds
1 teaspoon cumin seeds
¼ teaspoon chilli powder, or to taste
½ teaspoon fenugreek seeds
2 tablespoons butter
3 large parsnips, peeled and chopped
2 medium onions, chopped
2 cloves garlic, minced
sea salt
black pepper
1 cup cream
½ cup finely chopped coriander leaves

1 Combine the coriander seeds, cumin, chilli and fenugreek, and pound them in a mortar until well ground. Set aside. 2 Melt the butter in a large, heavy based saucepan over medium heat. Add the parsnip, onion and garlic, and sauté until softened. 3 Add just enough water to cover the parsnip and simmer for 20 minutes or until the parsnip is tender. 4 Remove from the heat and allow to cool. 5 Transfer the soup to a food processor or blender and process until smooth. Season to taste with salt and pepper. 6 Return the soup to the saucepan over medium heat and stir in the cream. 7 Serve immediately, sprinkled with the chopped coriander.

Serving idea
Serve with fried parsnip chips

2 tablespoons olive oil
24 green onion stalks, sliced thinly
2 cloves garlic, minced
1 tablespoon finely grated ginger
3 tablespoons cashews, dry-roasted
1 tablespoon sesame seeds, toasted
350 grams snow peas, stems and
     strings removed
1 teaspoon sesame oil
2 teaspoons soy sauce
cracked black pepper

1 Heat the olive oil in a wok or large frying pan over high heat. 2 Add the green onion, garlic and ginger, and sauté until just starting to sizzle. 3 Reduce the heat. Add the cashews and sesame seeds, and sauté for 1–2 minutes or until the onion and garlic are golden. 4 Add the snow peas and toss well. 5 Stir in the sesame oil and soy sauce, and stir-fry for 1 minute. 6 Remove from the heat and sprinkle generously with pepper. 7 Serve immediately.

Serving idea
Serve with grilled fish and Chilli Jam
recipe for Chilli and Tomato Jam, page 148

2 tablespoons butter
1 large onion, finely chopped
1 stalk celery, finely chopped
1 litre vegetable stock (recipe, page 152)
3 cups fresh peas, shelled
1 tablespoon finely chopped parsley
1 tablespoon finely chopped mint
sea salt
black pepper
250 grams short grain rice, steamed
100 ml sour cream

1 Melt the butter in a large saucepan or pot over medium heat. Add the onion and celery, and sauté until softened. 2 Pour in the stock and bring to the boil. 3 Add the peas, parsley and mint, and cook for 8–10 minutes. 4 Season to taste with salt and pepper. 5 Add the steamed rice and cook for a further 5 minutes. 6 Remove from the heat and ladle the soup into individual bowls. 7 Add a spoonful of sour cream and season with a grind of black pepper.

Serving idea
Top with grilled bacon

Buttered Peas
with Leek and Sage

3 cups peas
2 tablespoons butter
1 bunch sage
1 large leek, julienned
sea salt
black pepper

1 Bring a large saucepan of water to the boil. Add the peas and cook for 1–2 minutes or until just tender. 2 Rinse the peas under cold water and drain well. 3 Melt the butter in a frying pan over medium heat. Add the sage and leeks, and sauté for 3–4 minutes or until softened. 4 Add the peas and toss together for 30 seconds. 5 Remove from the heat and season generously with salt and pepper.

Serving idea
Serve with lemon-roasted chicken

1 kilogram sebago or spunt potatoes, washed
100 grams butter, at room temperature
1 cup cream, at room temperature
sea salt
black pepper

1 Preheat the oven to 220°C. 2 Prick the outsides of the potatoes and place on the rack in the preheated oven. 3 Roast for 1–1½ hours or until tender to the touch. 4 Remove from the oven and set aside to cool slightly. 5 Cut the potatoes in half and scoop out the centres. Discard the skins. 6 Mash the potatoes in a large bowl with a masher or pass through a food mill with large holes. 7 Stir in the butter and cream until you have a smooth consistency. 8 Season with salt and pepper, and serve immediately.

Serving idea
Serve with roast beef or lamb

Roasted Potato and Garlic with Rosemary

500 grams kipfler or waxy potatoes
1 head garlic, separated but not peeled
2 tablespoons olive oil
1 tablespoon rosemary leaves
2 sprigs thyme
sea salt
black pepper

1 Preheat the oven to 200°C. 2 Scrub the potatoes, slice in half lengthwise and place in a bowl of salted water for 10–15 minutes. 3 Drain and pat dry with absorbent kitchen paper. 4 Place the garlic, oil, rosemary and thyme in a baking dish, and toss with the potato. Season with salt and pepper. 5 Roast the potato for 25–30 minutes, turning several times, until the potato is tender and can be pierced with a knife. 6 Remove from the oven and serve immediately.

Serving idea
Serve with a Sunday roast

750 grams waxy potatoes, peeled
50 grams butter
2 cloves garlic, finely chopped
1 medium onion, finely chopped
salt
black pepper
200 ml milk
300 ml cream
1 teaspoon plain flour

1 Preheat the oven to 200°C. 2 Slice the potatoes thinly, using a mandolin if possible. 3 Grease a gratin dish with half the butter. Cover the base of the dish with a layer of slightly overlapping potato slices. 4 Dot the potato with a little butter. Sprinkle over a little onion and garlic, and season with salt and pepper. Repeat the layering process until all the ingredients are used. 5 Heat the milk in a saucepan over medium heat until warmed through. Remove from the heat. Add the cream and flour, and mix until smooth. 6 Carefully pour the liquid over the potato. 7 Bake for 1 hour or until the potato is soft and the top of the gratin is golden brown. 8 Serve hot.

Serving idea
Serve with roast beef

Spaghetti with Potato, Sage and Lemon

8 large potatoes, peeled
olive oil
1 large onion, sliced
3 cloves garlic, finely chopped
½ cup sage leaves
500 grams spaghetti
1½ cups vegetable stock (recipe, page 152)
sea salt
black pepper
juice of 1 large lemon
100 grams pecorino cheese, shaved

1 Preheat the oven to 200°C. 2 Thinly slice the potatoes, using a mandolin if possible. 3 Arrange the potato slices on 2 lightly oiled baking trays. 4 Drizzle with a little olive oil and bake for 15–20 minutes or until tender and golden. Set aside. 5 Add the spaghetti to a large saucepan of boiling water, and cook until al dente. 6 Heat 1 tablespoon of oil in a large pot over medium heat. Add the onion and garlic, and sauté until softened. 7 Add the sage and sauté for 1 minute or until soft. 8 Add the spaghetti and toss to combine. 9 Pour in the stock, season with salt and pepper, and toss together for 2 minutes. 10 Add the potato slices and lemon juice, and toss for 1 minute further or until the liquid has reduced. 11 Remove from the heat and drizzle with a little olive oil. 12 Transfer to a large serving platter and sprinkle with the pecorino.

Serving idea
Serve with rocket salad

2 large egg yolks, at room temperature
1 teaspoon Dijon mustard
2 tablespoons white wine vinegar
salt
white pepper
⅔ cup olive oil
1 teaspoon finely chopped garlic

500 grams waxy potatoes
200 grams green beans, trimmed
black pepper

1 For the mayonnaise, place the egg yolk, mustard, vinegar, salt and white pepper in a food processor or blender and process briefly until combined. 2 With the motor running, gradually pour in the olive oil until the mixture is thick and smooth. 3 Pour the mayonnaise into a bowl, and adjust seasonings to taste. 4 Pound the garlic and a little more salt in a mortar until smooth. 5 Stir into the mayonnaise and set aside. 6 Bring a large saucepan of water to the boil. Add the potatoes and simmer for 20−25 minutes or until tender. 7 Drain and allow to cool slightly. 8 Bring another saucepan of water to the boil. Add the beans and cook for 10 minutes or until just tender. 9 Refresh under cold water and drain. 10 Peel the potatoes and cut into large chunks. 11 Combine the potato and beans and spoon over some of the mayonnaise. 12 Season with black pepper and serve immediately.

Serving idea
**Serve with barbecued sausages
and spinach salad**

2 tablespoons olive oil

1 clove garlic, finely chopped

500 grams pumpkin, peeled and diced

sea salt

black pepper

3 tablespoons roughly chopped basil

1 cup cream

½ cup milk

100 grams Parmesan cheese, finely grated

1 Preheat the oven to 180°C. 2 Heat the oil in a frying pan over medium heat. Add the garlic and pumpkin, season with salt and pepper, and sauté for 5 minutes. 3 Arrange the pumpkin in a shallow gratin dish, and sprinkle over the chopped basil. 4 Heat the cream and milk in a saucepan over medium heat. Add the Parmesan and stir until the sauce thickens slightly. 5 Pour the sauce into the gratin dish until the pumpkin is almost covered. Season generously with pepper. 6 Bake for 25–30 minutes or until the pumpkin is tender and the top is golden.

Serving idea

Serve with lamb cutlets

100 grams yellow lentils
3 tablespoons vegetable oil
1 teaspoon mustard seeds
2 cloves garlic
1 teaspoon minced ginger
1 large onion, chopped
½ teaspoon turmeric
2 teaspoons red curry paste
3 large waxy potatoes, peeled and chopped
250 grams pumpkin, peeled and chopped
400 grams tinned tomatoes, chopped
1 cup coconut milk
salt
⅓ cup roughly chopped coriander leaves

1 Wash the lentils well in several changes of water. Drain and set aside. 2 Heat the oil in a large saucepan or pot over medium heat. 3 Add the mustard seeds. When they begin to pop, add the garlic, ginger, onion, turmeric and curry paste. 4 Sauté for 3–4 minutes or until the onion has just started to soften. 5 Add the potato and pumpkin, and toss to coat with the spices. 6 Add the tomato and lentils, and stir to combine well. You may need to add a little water if it is too thick. 7 Cover and simmer for 20–30 minutes or until the potato and pumpkin are tender. 8 Season to taste with salt. Add the coconut milk and simmer for a further 10 minutes. 9 To serve, ladle the curry into serving bowls and sprinkle over the coriander leaves.

Serving idea
Serve with basmati rice and naan

800 grams butternut pumpkin,
    peeled and chopped
1 head garlic, separated but not peeled
2 large onions, peeled and quartered
¼ cup olive oil
3 tablespoons balsamic vinegar
salt
black pepper
3 tablespoons roughly chopped parsley

1 Preheat the oven to 220°C. 2 Arrange the pumpkin, garlic and onion in a shallow baking dish. 3 Combine the oil and vinegar, drizzle over the vegetables and toss to coat well. 4 Season with salt and pepper and roast for 25 minutes. 5 Turn the pumpkin pieces over and roast for a further 15 minutes or until tender and golden. 6 To serve, arrange the vegetables on a serving platter, scatter over with parsley and season with black pepper.

Serving idea
Serve with braised beef

800 grams pumpkin, peeled and chopped
1 large egg
1 cup grams plain flour
100 grams Parmesan cheese, finely grated
1 pinch paprika
sea salt
black pepper
100 grams butter, diced
1 tablespoon lemon juice
2 tablespoons roughly chopped sage

1 Bring a large saucepan of water to the boil. Add the pumpkin and boil for 15 minutes or until tender. Drain well. 2 Mash the pumpkin thoroughly or pass through a food mill. 3 Place the mashed pumpkin in a bowl. Add the egg, flour, Parmesan and paprika. Season with salt and pepper. 4 Combine thoroughly until you have a soft dough. 5 Lightly dust a flat, dry surface with flour. Take a spoonful of the dough and work it into a small ball. 6 Press gently with a fork on one side to make a pattern. 7 Continue this process with the remaining dough. 8 Bring a large saucepan of water to the boil. Add some of the gnocchi and cook until they rise to the surface of the water. 9 Scoop out and drain. Cook the remaining gnocchi in batches. 10 Meanwhile, melt the butter in a frying pan over medium heat. Add the lemon juice and sage, and cook until golden. 11 To serve place the gnocchi in a serving bowl and pour over the sage butter.

Serving idea
Serve with grilled shellfish

500 grams pumpkin, peeled and chopped

olive oil

sea salt

black pepper

4 sprigs rosemary, picked

5 cups chicken or vegetable stock
(recipe, page 152)

1 cup dry white wine

2 tablespoons butter

1 small onion, finely chopped

2 cloves garlic

2 cups arborio rice

75 grams Parmesan cheese, finely grated

1 Preheat the oven to 220°C. 2 Place the pumpkin on a baking tray and drizzle with enough olive oil to coat the pumpkin. 3 Season with salt and pepper and sprinkle over half the rosemary. 4 Bake for 20 minutes or until tender. 5 Meanwhile, place the stock and wine in a large saucepan over medium heat and bring to a simmer. 6 Heat 1 tablespoon of oil and 1 tablespoon of the butter in another large, heavy based saucepan over medium heat. 7 Add the onion and garlic, and sauté until just soft. 8 Add the rice and coat well in the oils. Cook until the rice is translucent. 9 Add 1 cup of stock, stirring continuously until it has been absorbed. 10 Continue adding stock 1 cup at a time until the rice is soft and the consistency is creamy. 11 Add the cooked pumpkin and the remaining rosemary, and stir through. 12 When the risotto is almost cooked, stir through the remaining butter and the Parmesan. 13 Season to taste with salt and pepper.

Serving idea

Serve with baby spinach and tomato salad

Rocket and Tomato Salad
with Toasted Breadcrumbs

¼ cup olive oil plus 2 tablespoons extra
1 clove garlic, finely chopped
2 cups fresh, coarse breadcrumbs
250 grams baby rocket
100 grams baby spinach
4 medium Roma tomatoes, sliced
½ small lemon
sea salt
black pepper

1 Heat 2 tablespoons of the oil in a frying pan over medium heat. Add the garlic and sauté until golden. 2 Add the breadcrumbs and sauté until just golden. 3 Remove from the heat and allow to cool. 4 Combine the rocket, spinach and tomato in a salad bowl. 5 Add the remaining oil and a squeeze of lemon, and toss gently. 6 Sprinkle over the toasted breadcrumbs and season with salt and pepper.

Serving idea
Serve with crispy pancetta or bacon and eggs

Baby Spinach Salad
with Roasted Pumpkin and Olives

500 grams pumpkin, peeled and cut into
   2 cm cubes
3 tablespoons olive oil plus extra for roasting
sea salt
250 grams baby spinach
1 tablespoon finely chopped rosemary
10 Ligurian olives
black pepper

1 Preheat the oven to 200°C. 2 Place the pumpkin in a baking dish and toss well in olive oil. 3 Season with salt and roast for 30 minutes or until soft and golden. Set aside to cool. 4 Arrange the spinach on a serving plate and scatter over the roasted pumpkin. 5 Mix 3 tablespoons of oil with the rosemary, and pour over the spinach and pumpkin. 6 Scatter over the olives and season with salt and pepper.

Serving idea
Serve with couscous

6 tablespoons butter
juice of ½ small lemon
1 bunch English spinach, washed and
    stems trimmed
sea salt
black pepper
grated nutmeg

1 Melt the butter in a large pan over medium heat. Add the lemon juice and spinach leaves, and sauté until the spinach has just wilted. 2 Season with salt, pepper and nutmeg to taste. 3 Serve immediately.

Serving idea
Serve with roasted snapper

2 tablespoons butter
6 tablespoons olive oil
2 cloves garlic, minced
6 slices French bread, cubed
4 cups baby spinach leaves
1 bunch asparagus, blanched
60 grams Gruyère cheese, shaved
1 teaspoon sherry vinegar
1 pinch sugar

1 Preheat the oven to 180°C. 2 Heat the butter, 2 tablespoons of the oil and the garlic in a frying pan over medium heat until the butter is melted. 3 Add the bread cubes and toss until well coated in the oil. 4 Arrange the bread cubes in one layer on a baking tray and bake for 15 minutes or until browned and crisp. Set aside to cool. 5 Combine the spinach, asparagus and Gruyère in a bowl. Toss to combine. 6 Mix together the remaining oil, vinegar and sugar, and drizzle over the spinach salad. 7 Add the croutons and toss. 8 Serve immediately.

Serving idea
Serve with pancetta

Spinach and Orange Salad with Pine Nuts

1 large orange, peeled
4 cups baby spinach leaves, washed
1 large Spanish onion, finely sliced
1 teaspoon orange zest
¼ cup olive oil
¼ cup orange juice
1 tablespoon lemon juice
sea salt
black pepper
2 tablespoons pine nuts, toasted

1 Separate the orange segments and cut into small chunks. 2 Place the orange in a bowl with the spinach and onion. 3 Mix together the orange zest, olive oil, orange juice and lemon juice. 4 Season with salt and pepper, and pour over the spinach. Toss to combine. 5 To serve, sprinkle with the pine nuts.

Serving idea
Serve with cold roast chicken

Wilted Spinach
with Toasted Sesame Seeds

2 bunches spinach, washed and
  stems trimmed
1 piece konbu, about 6 cm
1 cup dried bonito flakes
1 tablespoon soy sauce
1 tablespoon rice vinegar
1 teaspoon dark sesame oil
2 tablespoons sesame seeds, toasted

1 Bring a large saucepan of water to the boil. Add the spinach leaves and cook for 1 minute or until the leaves have just wilted. 2 Remove and refresh under cold water. 3 Drain well and carefully separate the leaves. 4 Place 500 ml of fresh water in a saucepan. Add the konbu and slowly bring to a simmer. 5 Remove the konbu and add the bonito flakes. Slowly bring to the boil. 6 Once the liquid begins to boil, remove from the heat and strain through a fine-meshed sieve into a bowl. 7 Add the soy sauce, vinegar and sesame oil. Stir to combine. 8 Arrange the spinach leaves on a serving plate, pour over the sauce and sprinkle with the toasted sesame seeds. 9 Serve immediately.

Serving idea
Serve with grilled fish

800 grams sweet potato, peeled and chopped
100 grams butter, chopped
¾ cup cream
½ teaspoon cinnamon
sea salt
pepper

1 Bring a large saucepan of water to the boil. Add the sweet potato and cook for 15 minutes or until tender. Drain. 2 Mash the sweet potato in a large bowl with a potato masher or pass through a food mill with large holes. 3 Stir in the butter and cream until you have a smooth consistency. 4 Season with cinnamon, salt and pepper, and serve immediately.

Serving idea
Serve with honey-roasted ham

Curried Sweet Potato and Apple Soup

3 tablespoons butter
1 small onion, finely chopped
2 cloves garlic, finely chopped
1 stick celery, finely chopped
1 teaspoon Indian curry paste, or to taste
1 kilogram sweet potato, peeled and chopped
salt
pepper
3 cups vegetable stock (recipe, page 152)
3 small green apples, peeled and chopped
1 cup cream

1 Melt the butter in a large, heavy based pot over medium heat. 2 Add the onion, garlic and celery, and sauté until softened. 3 Add the curry paste and sauté for 1–2 minutes. 4 Add the sweet potato, season with salt and pepper, and sauté for 4–5 minutes. 5 Pour in the stock. 6 Add the apple and simmer for 15 minutes or until the sweet potato is tender. 7 Remove from the heat and allow to cool. 8 In batches, transfer the mixture to a food processor and blend until smooth. 9 Return the soup to the pan and adjust seasonings to taste. 10 Stir in the cream and cook until the soup is simmering. 11 Serve immediately with a good grind of pepper.

Serving idea
Serve with sourdough bread

4 tablespoons butter
2 tablespoons finely chopped oregano
800 grams sweet potato, peeled and chopped
4 tablespoons honey

1 Preheat the oven to 220°C. 2 Melt the butter in a pan over medium heat. 3 Add the oregano and sauté until just softened. 4 Arrange the sweet potato in a baking dish large enough to hold it in one layer. 5 Drizzle over the butter and oregano, and toss to coat well. 6 Roast for 15 minutes. 7 Add the honey and toss to coat well. 8 Roast for a further 10–15 minutes or until tender and slightly browned. 9 Serve immediately.

Serving idea
Serve with roast turkey

Sweet Potato Pancakes
with Yoghurt Dressing

800 grams sweet potato, peeled and chopped
2 large eggs, beaten
1 small onion, grated
2 tablespoons butter, melted,
    plus extra for frying
½ cup plain flour
1 teaspoon curry powder
½ teaspoon cinnamon
1 pinch salt

½ cup plain yogurt
2 teaspoons cumin
1 tablespoon honey

1 Bring a large saucepan of water to the boil. Add the sweet potato and cook for 15 minutes or until tender. Drain well. 2 Mash the sweet potato with a potato masher in a large bowl or pass through a food mill with large holes. 3 Add the egg and combine. 4 Pat the grated onion with absorbent kitchen paper to soak up any excess liquid. 5 Add the onion, 2 tablespoons of butter, the flour, curry powder, cinnamon and salt to the bowl, and stir to combine well. 6 Spoon out the sweet potato mixture to form patties. Flatten each patty to make a pancake 5 mm thick and 8 cm in diameter. 7 Melt some butter in a non-stick frying pan over medium heat. 8 Add the pancakes 2 or 3 at a time and cook for 2 minutes each side or until golden brown. 9 For the dressing, combine the yoghurt, cumin and honey. 10 To serve, arrange the pancakes on a serving plate and spoon over the yoghurt dressing.

Serving idea
Serve with steamed green beans

Sweet Potato Salad
with Chilli and Ginger

800 grams sweet potato, peeled
3 tablespoons olive oil plus extra for roasting
salt
black pepper
4 green onions, sliced
3 tablespoons sweet chilli sauce
1 tablespoon ginger, minced
1 tablespoon lemon juice

1 Preheat the oven to 200°C. 2 Cut the sweet potato into large slices and place in a baking dish. 3 Drizzle with olive oil and season with salt and pepper. Toss to coat in the oil. 4 Roast for 25–30 minutes or until tender and golden. 5 Arrange the roasted sweet potato on a serving plate and scatter with green onion. 6 For the dressing, combine the sweet chilli sauce, ginger, lemon juice and 3 tablespoons of olive oil. 7 Spoon the dressing over the sweet potatoes and serve immediately.

Serving idea
Serve with stir-fried beef

1 cup basil leaves
2 cloves garlic, chopped
2 sprigs thyme, chopped
1 pinch sugar
½ cup olive oil
sea salt
black pepper
8 medium Roma tomatoes, quartered

1 Preheat the oven to 60°C. 2 Place the basil, garlic, thyme and sugar in a food processor and process until finely chopped. With the motor running, gradually pour in the olive oil and process until smooth. 3 Season to taste with salt and pepper. 4 Place the quartered tomatoes on a rack inside an oven tray. 5 Brush the basil mixture generously over the tomatoes. 6 Cook for 3 hours or until the tomatoes have softened and shrivelled slightly.

Serving idea
Serve with barbecued steak or sausages

200 grams baby spinach leaves
2 medium Spanish onions, sliced
1 punnet cherry tomatoes, cut into halves
100 grams ricotta cheese
juice of ½ medium lemon
olive oil for drizzling
sea salt
black pepper

1 Wash the spinach leaves and drain well.
2 Place the onion, tomato and ricotta in a bowl and toss together gently. 3 Place the spinach leaves on a serving platter. Top with the onion, tomato and ricotta mixture. 4 Squeeze over the lemon juice. 5 Drizzle with olive oil and season with salt and pepper.

Serving idea
Serve with cured meats and antipasto

2 tablespoons olive oil

1 medium onion, finely chopped

3 cloves garlic, minced

2 x 440 gram tins of tomatoes,
    drained and chopped

½ cup roughly chopped basil leaves

3 small fennel bulbs, trimmed

1 cup vegetable stock (recipe, page 152)

sea salt

black pepper

40 grams Parmesan cheese, finely grated

1 Preheat the oven to 180°C. 2 Heat the oil in a large, heavy based saucepan over a medium heat. Add the onion and garlic, and cook until softened. 3 Add the tomatoes and simmer for 15 minutes, stirring occasionally. 4 Add the basil and simmer for 5–10 minutes or until the sauce has thickened. 5 Cut the fennel bulbs in half lengthwise, and then cut each half into 4 pieces. 6 Place the fennel and stock into a large pot or casserole over medium heat. Cover and simmer for 10–15 minutes or until the fennel begins to soften. 7 Remove the lid, increase the heat and cook until the liquid has evaporated. Gently shake the pot to prevent the fennel from sticking. 8 Remove from the heat and season with salt and pepper. 9 Transfer the fennel to a baking dish large enough to hold the fennel in a single layer. 10 Pour the tomato and basil sauce over the fennel, and sprinkle with Parmesan. 11 Cook in the oven for 15–20 minutes or until the cheese has browned and the sauce is bubbling. 12 Serve immediately.

Serving idea

Serve with sautéed red mullet

3 medium turnips, peeled and quartered
2 medium carrots, peeled and chopped
1 x 6 cm piece konbu
1 small leek, finely sliced
1 cup bonito flakes
3 tablespoons red miso paste
2 medium zucchini, chopped
4 stalks green onion, halved and thinly sliced
sansho powder for seasoning

1 Bring a large saucepan of water to the boil. Add the turnip and carrot and cook for 10 minutes or until just tender. 2 Drain well. 3 In another saucepan, add 1.5 litres of water and the konbu and slowly bring to a simmer. 4 As soon as the water is simmering, remove the konbu and discard. 5 Add the leek and bonito flakes. Slowly bring to the boil. 6 Once the liquid begins to boil, remove from the heat and strain through a fine-meshed sieve and into a heat-proof bowl. 7 Discard the contents of the sieve. 8 Return the strained liquid to the saucepan. 9 Mix the miso paste with a little water so it has a runny consistency. Stir in the miso and zucchini. 10 Simmer over medium heat for 5 minutes or until the zucchini is just tender. 11 Place equal portions of the turnip and carrot into soup bowls. 12 Ladle the miso soup into the bowls. Garnish with green onion and season with sansho powder.

Serving idea
Serve with salmon poached in the soup

Roasted Baby Turnips with Parsley Oil

12 small turnips, trimmed and peeled
2 tablespoons olive oil for drizzling
salt
cracked black pepper
¼ cup parsley leaves
1 clove garlic
½ cup olive oil
100 grams Gruyère cheese, finely grated

1 Preheat the oven to 200°C. 2 Cut the turnips into quarters and arrange in a shallow roasting pan. Drizzle over some olive oil and toss to coat well. 3 Season with salt and pepper, and roast for 25–30 minutes or until tender. 4 Meanwhile, place the parsley and garlic in a food processor and process until finely chopped. 5 With the motor running, gradually pour in the olive oil and process until smooth. 6 Season to taste with salt and pepper. 7 Pour into a container and set aside. 8 When the turnip is done, remove it from the oven and arrange on a serving plate. 9 Drizzle with parsley oil and sprinkle with Gruyère shavings and pepper.

Serving idea
Serve with beef casserole

1 cup vegetable stock (recipe, page 152)

2 tablespoons butter

12 small turnips, trimmed, peeled and cut
into quarters

1 tablespoon sugar

salt

pepper

2 tablespoons finely chopped parsley

1 Heat the stock in a saucepan over medium–high heat. 2 Melt the butter in a second, larger saucepan over medium heat. Add the turnip and toss to coat in the butter. 3 Sprinkle over the sugar and stir until golden. 4 Slowly pour in the stock and season with salt and pepper. Cover and simmer for 10–15 minutes or until the turnip is tender. 5 If there is still some liquid in the pan, increase the heat to quickly evaporate the liquid. 6 Add the parsley and toss the turnip pieces until they are lightly browned. 7 Serve immediately.

Serving idea

Serve with sausages and mashed potato

6 medium witlof
2 tablespoons butter
juice of ½ lemon, plus 2 small lemons,
    quartered
½ cup kalamata olives, pitted
1 cup white wine
2 cups vegetable stock (recipe, page 152)
sea salt
white pepper
chopped parsley for serving
black pepper for serving

1 Preheat the oven to 180°C. 2 Remove any dark or wilted outer leaves from the witlof and discard. 3 Slice the witlof in half lengthwise and arrange in a baking dish large enough to hold the witlof in one layer. 4 Melt the butter in a pan, add the lemon juice and pour over the witlof. 5 Toss the witlof in the butter to coat well. 6 Scatter over the olives and lemon quarters. 7 Pour over the wine and stock and season with salt and pepper. 8 Cover with aluminium foil and bake for 20 minutes. 9 Remove briefly from the oven to turn over the witlof. 10 Return to the oven uncovered and bake for a further 10 minutes or until the witlof is tender and the liquid has reduced. 11 To serve, place the witlof on a serving plate and spoon over the olives, lemon and a little of the liquid. 12 Sprinkle over chopped parsley and black pepper and serve immediately.

Serving idea
Serve with roasted breast of squab

Grilled Witlof with Lemon and Walnut Dressing

4 large witlof
5 tablespoons olive oil
1 cup dry white wine
2 cups vegetable stock (recipe, page 152)
sea salt
black pepper

50 grams walnuts, finely chopped
1 small lemon, juiced
1 teaspoon Dijon mustard
1 tablespoon walnut oil

1 Preheat the oven to 180°C. 2 Remove any dark or wilted outer leaves from the witlof and discard. 3 Place the witlof in a baking dish and toss with 2 tablespoons of the olive oil. 4 Add the wine and stock, and season with salt and pepper. 5 Cover and bake for 25 minutes, turning once or twice. 6 Remove from the oven, discard the liquid and set aside to cool or refrigerate overnight. 7 Preheat the grill to medium. 8 When ready to use, cut the witlof in half lengthwise and brush with the remaining olive oil. 9 Grill on a barbecue or grill plate for 5 minutes or until the outside of the witlof is golden brown. 10 Set aside. 11 Place the chopped walnuts, lemon juice, Dijon mustard and walnut oil in a bowl and mix together until thoroughly combined. 12 Season to taste with salt and pepper. 13 To serve, arrange the grilled witlof on a serving plate and spoon over the dressing.

Serving idea
Serve with barbecued fish

2 medium witlof
2 bunches watercress,
    washed and stalks removed
1 medium avocado, peeled and sliced
⅓ cup olive oil
3 tablespoons orange juice
½ teaspoon orange zest
1 teaspoon balsamic vinegar
sea salt
black pepper

1 Remove any dark or wilted outer leaves from the witlof and discard. 2 Separate the witlof leaves and discard the hard core. Slice the leaves into strips lengthwise. 3 Combine the witlof, watercress and avocado in a serving bowl. 4 For the dressing, stir the olive oil, orange juice, orange zest and balsamic vinegar in a bowl. Season with salt and pepper. 5 Pour the dressing over the leaves and toss together gently.

Serving idea
Serve with leftover roast chicken

Pasta with Zucchini, Chilli, Capers and Lemon

400 grams spaghetti
2 tablespoons olive oil
2 tablespoons chilli oil (recipe, page 147)
2 cloves garlic, finely chopped
5 medium zucchini, thinly sliced
1 tablespoon capers, rinsed
juice of 1 small lemon
½ cup roughly chopped basil

1 Bring a large saucepan of water to the boil. Add the spaghetti and cook for 8 minutes or until al dente. 2 Drain well and set aside. 3 Heat the olive oil and chilli oil in a large frying pan over medium heat. Add the garlic and sauté for 1–2 minutes or until the garlic just starts to sizzle. 4 Add the zucchini and capers, and cook for 2 minutes or until the zucchini is just golden. 5 Add the pasta to the pan and toss well to coat. 6 Add the lemon juice and basil, and toss well in the pan. 7 Serve immediately.

Serving idea
Serve with green salad leaves

Roasted Zucchini
with Lemon and Mint

6 large zucchini
3 tablespoons grapeseed oil
sea salt
juice of 1 small lemon
2 tablespoons orange juice
2 tablespoons finely chopped mint
black pepper

1 Preheat the oven to 180°C. 2 Trim the ends from the unpeeled zucchini, slice in half lengthwise, and cut across in half again. 3 Arrange the zucchini in a roasting pan and toss in half (1½ tablespoons) of the oil. 4 Season with salt and roast for 10 minutes. Shake the pan a couple of times while roasting. 5 Remove from the oven and set aside to cool. 6 In a bowl, combine the lemon juice, orange juice, mint and remaining oil. 7 Transfer the zucchini to a serving bowl, spoon over the dressing and toss to combine. 8 Serve with a good grind of black pepper.

Serving idea
Serve with Roasted Tomatoes
recipe, page 131

6 medium zucchini, grated to make 2 cups
½ cup plain flour
3 large eggs, lightly beaten
1 clove garlic, minced
15 grams Parmesan cheese, finely grated
2 tablespoons finely chopped basil
salt
pepper
olive oil for frying

1 Place the grated zucchini in a bowl and add the flour, eggs, garlic, Parmesan cheese and basil. 2 Season with salt and pepper, and combine well. 3 Make patties by spooning out the zucchini mixture, forming it into balls and flattening them with your hands. 4 Pour oil into a frying pan to a depth of 1 cm. Heat over medium heat. Place one patty in the hot oil and fry until a golden crust has formed on the first side. Turn over and fry the other side. 5 Repeat for the remaining patties and serve immediately.

Serving idea
Serve with brie and tomato

Balsamic Dressing

4 cloves garlic, minced
5 tablespoons balsamic vinegar
5 tablespoons olive oil
sea salt
black pepper

Combine all the ingredients in a bowl.

Chilli Oil

1 cup olive oil
3 small red chillies, chopped
½ cup finely chopped basil leaves
10 whole black peppercorns

1 Combine all the ingredients in a small bowl. Pour the mixture into a glass bottle and set aside to infuse for at least 1 hour. 2 Cover and refrigerate until ready to use.

Serving idea
Pour over your favourite roasted or grilled vegetables

Serving idea
Serve drizzled over fresh pasta

Chilli and Tomato Jam

1 kilogram tomatoes, halved
5 tablespoons olive oil
4 cloves garlic, chopped
1 teaspoon minced ginger
4 small red chillies, chopped
1 teaspoon cumin seeds
1 teaspoon mustard seeds
5 tablespoons cider vinegar
5 teaspoons fish sauce
125 grams sugar
1 teaspoon turmeric
¼ cup finely chopped coriander

1 Preheat the oven to 180°C. 2 Place the tomato halves in a roasting tin and drizzle over the olive oil. 3 Roast the tomatoes for 25 minutes or until softened. 4 Place the garlic, ginger, chillies, cumin seeds, mustard seeds and vinegar in a food processor, and process until smooth. 5 Transfer the mixture to a heavy based saucepan and add the roasted tomato, fish sauce, sugar and turmeric. 6 Slowly bring to the boil, then simmer for 1½ hours or until thickened. 7 Stir in the chopped coriander and set aside to cool. 8 Pour into a storage container and refrigerate until ready to use.

Serving idea
Serve with grilled fish or meat

Moroccan Green Sauce

½ cup olive oil
juice of 1 large lemon
4 cloves garlic, minced
¾ cup finely chopped coriander
¼ cup finely chopped parsley
2 teaspoons paprika
1 teaspoon cumin
1 pinch cayenne pepper or to taste
salt

Process all the ingredients in a food
processor until smooth.

Mustard Butter

100 grams butter
2 cloves garlic
1 tablespoon Dijon mustard
1 stalk green onion, finely chopped
1 tablespoon finely chopped parsley
sea salt
black pepper

1 Melt the butter in a pan over medium heat.
Add the garlic and sauté until softened.
2 Add the remaining ingredients and stir to
combine well.

Serving idea
**Serve as a spicy addition to any sweet
roasted or grilled vegetables**

Serving idea
**Spoon over cabbage or other green
vegetables**

Olive Tapenade

200 grams kalamata olives,
    pitted and chopped
2 tablespoons capers, rinsed and chopped
2 cloves garlic, minced
1 tablespoon thyme leaves, finely chopped
5 tablespoons extra virgin olive oil
1 tablespoon lemon juice
black pepper

1 Place the olives, capers, garlic and thyme in a food processor, and process until finely chopped. 2 With the motor running, gradually pour in the olive oil and lemon juice and process until smooth. 3 Season to taste with black pepper.

Rich Garlic Mayonnaise

5 cloves garlic, chopped
sea salt
2 large egg yolks
2 cups extra virgin olive oil
2 tablespoons lemon juice

1 Place the garlic, salt and egg yolks in a blender or food processor and process until combined. 2 With the motor running, gradually pour in the olive oil and lemon juice and process until smooth.

Serving idea
Spread on eggplant or any other grilled vegetable

Serving idea
Serve drizzled over any vegetables

Rosemary and Garlic Pesto

¼ cup rosemary leaves
¼ cup chopped parsley leaves
2 cloves garlic, chopped
½ cup pine nuts
⅓ cup olive oil
sea salt
black pepper

1 Place the rosemary, parsley, garlic and pine nuts in a food processor and process until a paste is formed. 2 With the motor running, gradually pour in the olive oil and process until smooth. 3 Season to taste with salt and pepper.

Saffron Butter

1 pinch saffron
1 tablespoon warm water
100 grams unsalted butter at
    room temperature
1 tablespoon finely chopped parsley
1 pinch cayenne pepper
salt
white pepper

1 Place the saffron in a small bowl with the warm water and let stand for 10 minutes. 2 Combine all the ingredients, cover and refrigerate until ready to use.

Serving idea
Serve over any hot vegetables

Serving idea
Melt over warm potatoes or fennel

Sesame Soy Dressing

3 tablespoons light soy sauce
½ teaspoon minced garlic
1 tablespoon dark sesame oil
2 tablespoons olive oil
1 green onion, finely chopped

Combine all the ingredients in a bowl.

Vegetable Stock

2 tablespoons olive oil
500 grams chopped onion
250 grams chopped carrot
2 large leeks, chopped
2 stalks celery, chopped
5 cloves garlic, minced
½ bunch parsley, roughly chopped
2 sprigs thyme
3 bay leaves, whole
6 black peppercorns
sea salt

1 Heat the oil in a large saucepan or pot over medium heat. Add the onion, carrot, leek and celery, and sauté for 5 minutes. 2 Add the remaining ingredients and 2 litres of water and slowly bring to the boil. Simmer for 1 hour. 3 Remove from the heat and set aside to cool. 4 Strain through a fine-meshed sieve into a bowl. 5 Refrigerate for 2–3 days, or freeze in convenient portions.

Serving idea
Drizzle over any steamed green vegetable

Yoghurt Sauce

1 cup yoghurt
1 clove garlic, minced
1 small cucumber, finely diced
1 small tomato, finely diced
1 small green onion, finely chopped
1 tablespoon finely chopped parsley
1 tablespoon finely chopped mint (optional)
1 tablespoon olive oil

Combine all the ingredients in a small bowl.

Serving idea
**Serve to the side or spooned over any
cooked vegetables**

Bonito is a fish belonging to the mackeral family. Its dried flesh is flaked and used to add flavour in Japanese cookery. Available from Asian grocers.

Buffalo mozzarella is the most prized of all mozzarella cheeses. It is made from a combination of water buffalo milk and cow's milk, and is available from good delicatessens.

Fermented black beans, also known as Chinese black beans, are made from small black soy beans preserved in salt. They have a pungent and salty flavour and are usually chopped finely before being added to dishes. Available from Asian grocers and some supermarkets.

Haloumi is a stringy and salty cheese made from goat's milk. Haloumi can be cut into slices and grilled or fried in a little oil. Available from good delicatessens and supermarkets.

Hijiki is a type of Japanese seaweed that is sun-dried then boiled and dried again. It is black and stringy in appearance with a salty and slightly aniseed flavour. Available from Asian grocers.

Konbu is dried kelp used to make dashi (Japanese soup stock). When using konbu, wipe the surface gently with a damp cloth rather than washing it, as washing will remove the flavour. Store for up to six months in a cool, dry place. Available in long sheets or smaller pieces from Asian supermarkets.

Mirin also known as Japanese rice wine, is a sweet-flavoured liquid made from steamed glutinous rice and alcohol. Available from Asian grocers and the gourmet section of some supermarkets.

Miso is a fermented paste made from soy beans. Red miso paste is made from barley and soy beans, whereas white miso is made from rice and soy beans. Usually prepared as miso soup, this Japanese staple is highly nutritious. Available from Asian grocers, large supermarkets and health-food shops.

Parma ham is the true prosciutto, from the Italian province of Parma. Pigs are fed a special diet of chestnuts and whey, and the hams are seasoned, salt-cured and air-dried, but not smoked. Parma ham has a reddish-brown flesh that is firm and dense. Available from good delicatessans and supermarkets.

Parmigiana Reggiano is a cheese produced in the Italian regions of Bologna, Mantua, Modena and Parma. It is usually aged for more than two years, and has a complex flavour and a granular texture that melts in the mouth. Available from good delicatessans and supermarkets.

Red curry paste is a hot and spicy paste made from ground red chillies, aromatic herbs and spices. Available from Asian grocers and most supermarkets.

Saffron comes from the dried stigmas of the purple crocus flower. It is the world's most expensive spice, as it takes up to 200,000 stigmas to produce one kilogram of saffron. Commonly used in paella, bouillabaisse and risotto. Available in threads (whole stigmas) or in powder form from delicatessens and good supermarkets.

Sansho is an aromatic Japanese pepper made from the berries of the prickly ash tree. Sansho is usually bought ground and is closely related to the Chinese Sichuan pepper. Available from Asian supermarkets.

Sesame seeds are native to India and come in shades of black and brown, as well as the more common pale cream or white. Black seeds can be substituted for white seeds. Available at Asian grocers and supermarkets.

Shiitake mushrooms were first cultivated in Japan and Korea. The caps are dark brown, with a pale cream underside. The meaty flesh has a distinctive steak-like flavour. The stems tend to be a little tough, but are ideal to use in stocks. Available fresh from good fruit and vegetable stores. Dried shiitake mushrooms should be soaked in warm water for at least 30 minutes.

Soba noodles are Japanese noodles made from buckwheat and wheat flour. Great in soups or served cold. Available from Asian supermarkets.

Taleggio is semi-soft cheese from Italy's Lombardy region. As the cheese ages it becomes quite runny, the colour darkens and the flavour changes from mild to pungent. It is sold with a wax coating or in a thin mould. Available from good delicatessans and supermarkets.

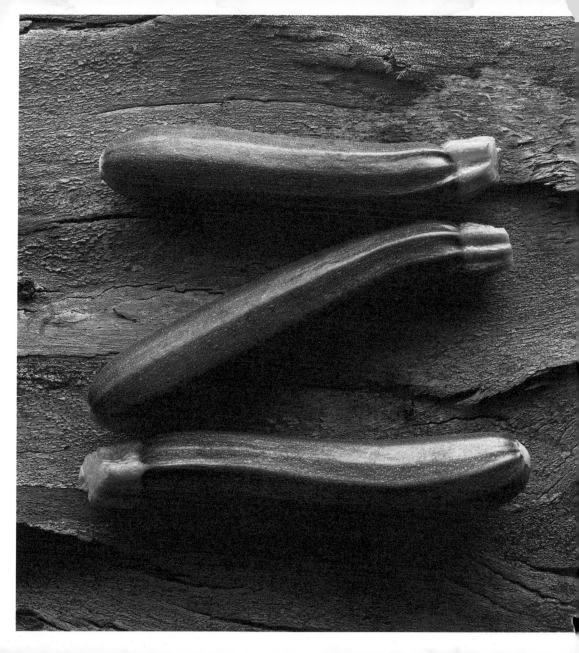